The Story of the Steiff Teddy Bear

The Story of the Steiff Teddy Bear

AN ILLUSTRATED HISTORY FROM 1902

Günther Pfeiffer

David & Charles

A DAVID & CHARLES BOOK

First published in the UK in 2003

© Originally published in German by HEEL Verlag GmbH,
Gut Pottscheidt, 53639 Königswinter, Germany, under licence
of Margarete Steiff GmbH, Giengen an der Brenz, 2002.

Translation by PS Translation, Germersheim/Germany

Distributed in North America
by F&W Publications, Inc.
4700 East Galbraith Road
Cincinnati, OH 45236
1-800-289-0963

A catalogue record for this book is available from the
British Library.

ISBN 0 7153 1606 0 paperback

Printed in China by Dai Nippon
for David & Charles
Brunel House   Newton Abbot   Devon

Visit our website at www.davidandcharles.co.uk

David & Charles books are available from all good bookshops;
alternatively you can contact our Orderline on (0)1626 334555
or write to us at FREEPOST EX2 110, David & Charles
Direct, Newton Abbot, TQ12 4ZZ (no stamp required
UK mainland).

Contents

Fig. 1: The oldest known jointed bear
that has survived the passage of time
is the 35PB dating back to 1904.

Foreword

The Teddy bear celebrates

its centenary in the year 2002

The main figure in one of the really great success stories of our time, he doesn't appear to have much in common with conventional modern heroes at first glance. Always calm and unassuming, he only raises his voice when explicitly asked to do so. He hardly has any needs of his own, but he's always there when we need him. These are qualities that are only characteristic of a real friend. And that – and much, much more – is exactly what our Teddy is.

It goes without saying that no reference to the Teddy would be complete without mentioning Margarete Steiff and her nephew, Richard Steiff, in the same breath. The story of Margarete Steiff's life and the history of the current Margarete Steiff GmbH that began in 1880 have been related in great detail and appropriately honoured in many films, books and other publications. The main figure in this book is the Teddy bear. The founder of the toy manufacturing establishment and the creator of the first jointed bear are therefore only mentioned on these pages in direct connection with the Teddy bear and in the context of historical events.

100 years of Steiff Teddy bears – a good enough reason to take a closer look at the story of Teddy's creation and his development over the last century.

Our congratulations on this special birthday!

Günther Pfeiffer

I. Richard Steiff's Idea

MOVABLE AND NATURAL-LOOKING
THAT IS WHAT THE NEW TOY SHOULD
BE LIKE, ALMOST ALIVE, IN FACT.
A BEAR LIKE THOSE IN THE ZOO OR
AT THE CIRCUS WOULD BE BEST.

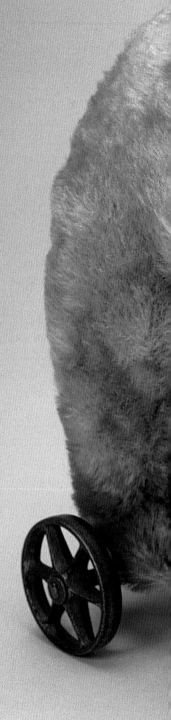

Fig. 2: A 35-cm tall bear on
wheels made of brown mohair
plush – Richard Steiff wants
greater movability.

Fig. 3: An outing on the ice –
in the fashion of the time.

It's 1902 and we have entered an age of respectability similar to that of post-Victorian England. The strictness of this epoch and all of its taboos are reflected in the fashion of the day. Ladies gowns are buttoned right up to the neck, with skirts that touch the ground and laced-in waistlines, and the men's fashions are similarly austere.

The first street lanterns are also being installed in the larger cities now, however. And although the few motor-cars driving along the roads are still very reminiscent of horse-drawn carriages, they are a clear indication of the progress to come. In America, for example, the Wright brothers are making their first attempts to take to the skies with their motor-driven flying machines. Art Nouveau is setting the tone for development in the history of art. Henri de Toulouse-Lautrec, Emile Gallé, Gustav Klimt and Franz von Stuck are significant representatives of this period.

Richard Steiff also embodies the modern, young spirit of the turn of the century, bubbling over with creativity and a wealth of ideas, with a completely open mind regarding all new developments.

Just 25 years old, this young man comes up with a sensational invention in the small town of Giengen an der Brenz. He designs and develops the very first jointed bear, the prototype of today's Teddy bear.

While studying at the school of art in Stuttgart, Richard produces a wealth of animal sketches during his frequent visits to the city's zoo. Apart from the brown bears, his favourite subjects, all types of other animals appear in the sketchbooks from that time that have been preserved in the Steiff archives. He paid particular attention to posture and movement and captured these as realistically as possible in numerous detailed drawings. Studying these illustrations, one is very much aware of his perpetual endeavours to get as close to the animals' natural lightness and motion as possible.

Fig. 4

Richard Steiff – The man

Richard first saw the light of day on February 7th, 1877, the second son born to master builder Fritz Steiff and his wife, Anna, née Böckh. He is the first of Margarete Steiff's nephews to join the staff of her felt business in 1897 in which he has played an active role since his youth.

Having completed his studies, he leaves art school in Stuttgart in 1897. In the same year, one of his first duties working for the "Margarete Steiff Filzspielwarenfabrik" [Margarete Steiff felt toy manufacturing establishment] is to represent the company during its first appearance at the Leipzig Spring Trade Fair.

A year later, Richard is sent to England in order to expand the firm's export business. On his return, he devotes all of his time to designing and manufacturing soft-filled toys. The 1902 catalogue already offers around 750 different articles, not allowing for the different colour schemes available for the various animals. Richard Steiff is the originator of many of the ideas and designs published in the catalogue.

Fig. 5: "Bear-driver with brown bear" was the name of a new article presented in 1899, which was modelled on this drawing signed by Margarete Steiff on 30th May 1899.

Fig. 6: A milestone of its day – the Mercedes Simplex.

11

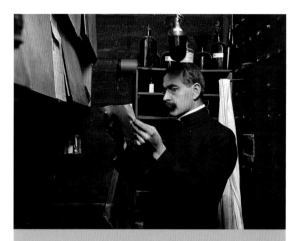

Fig. 7: Richard Steiff, the designer, in his studio.

Richard Steiff – The inventor

Richard Steiff lays the foundation stone for two other masterly achievements in 1902. The plan takes shape in his head and his hands produce drawings of the new factory building: made of glass and metal, a revolutionary construction in its day. The dates 1903, 1904 and 1908 inscribed on the walls still bear witness to the history of the premises, which are now scheduled as ancient monuments.

However, the invention that is much more important as far as we are concerned is the first bear with moving head and limbs. This bear, who has since become better known as the Teddy bear, was developed by Richard Steiff in Giengen in 1902 and set off on his voyage of world conquest in 1903. He deserves to be named after no less a person than the American president who is currently in office (but more about that later ...).

Richard's wealth of ideas seems to be inexhaustible. This is demonstrated by the Steiff kite Roloplan, for example, that he develops in 1908, or the important mechanical showpieces that emerge over the following years later as a result of his co-operation with Schlopsnies, the artist. Richard moves to America in the mid-1920s, where he continues his work, industriously creating new products or perfecting existing ones until his death in 1938.

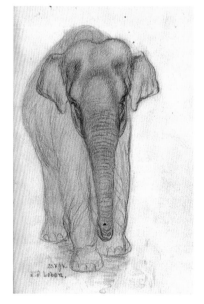

Abb. 9

Figs. 8-10: Illustrations from Richard Steiff's sketchbook.

Abb. 10

Fig. 11: Movable, but not dynamic
enough for Richard Steiff.

It isn't long before Richard tries to project his knowledge into production of the toys designed and manufactured in the factory of his aunt, Margarete Steiff. Even the animals on wheels, or those that could be set in motion by means of brushes or hemispherical bases are not dynamic enough for him.

What Richard Steiff is looking for is natural movement – he wants to breathe life into his toy animals. And he already has the possibility of realising this idea in his mind's eye: children playing with a naturally moving toy animal.

A brilliant idea, because the ideal children's toy created from this idea will guarantee sustained sales success for the toy factory on a long-term basis.

Fig. 12: Margarete Steiff in her youth (small photograph at the top),
Fig. 13: the businesswomen (underneath),
Fig. 14: with a Teddy (left).

Fig. 15: The house where Margarete Steiff was born.

Margarete Steiff

Childhood and youth

Apollonia Margarete Steiff is born on 24th July 1847 in Giengen an der Brenz. Her parents are Friedrich Steiff, master builder, and his wife, Maria Margarete, née Hähnle. Named after her mother, Margarete has two sisters, Marie and Pauline, who are just slightly older than herself, and a brother called Fritz, who is nearly 1½ years younger than she is. At the age of just 18 months, Margarete Steiff is taken ill with polio in December 1848/ January 1849. All attempts to heal the disease are in vain. It leaves her with a completely paralysed left foot and a partially paralysed right foot. Her right arm is also very weak. Margarete will spend the rest of her life in a wheelchair. She is a very vivacious little girl in spite of her disability and has no problems at all getting along with other children. Leaving school in 1861, Margarete is looking forward into a very uncertain future because the only thing she can do well is to sew – contributing towards her family's livelihood with her talented fingers. Margarete learns to play the zither and can eventually play so well that she can give lessons herself later in life. She goes to the sewing school in Giengen to learn her trade from the bottom up, and perfects her sewing skills. She saves the money earned with sewing jobs and playing the zither, and it accumulates so quickly that she is able to purchase a sewing machine as early as 1863. This enables her to complete her sewing jobs much more quickly and the number of orders soon increases, as well as her income.

The first years in business

Margarete's parents celebrate her 27th birthday on 24th July 1874 by giving her a separate apartment in the parental home. She uses this to open her own sewing company and 1877 sees her establishing a ready-to-wear felt clothing business. She is supported in her venture by Adolph Glatz, the husband of her cousin Marie. The positive relationships established between Margarete and the

"Württembergische Woll-Filz-Manufaktur Giengen" [Württembergian wool and felt article making company in Giengen], founded by her step-cousins Hans and Melchior Hähnle in 1866, enable her to carry out orders very quickly and she soon takes on several members of staff. In 1879, Margarete Steiff is flicking through a journal entitled "Die Modenwelt" [The World of Fashion] when she comes across a pattern and instructions for the production of a toy elephant made of fabric and filled with tow. She makes her elephant in accordance with these instructions, using felt for the body and shearing flock or felt trimmings for the filling – to produce the very first soft-filled toy animal. The first eight elephants that she produces are sold as early as 1880, the year in which today's Margarete Steiff GmbH is founded. Business increases continuously over the following years, not least thanks to the active support given by Fritz, Margarete's brother. The first riding and moving animals are manufactured as early as 1886. And a new home with business premises is built in Giengen just two years later. 1892 sees the publication of the very first toy catalogue, which already contains the motto still used for the products of Margarete Steiff GmbH today: "Only the best is good enough for children!". A trademark is used to distinguish Steiff products from those of rival firms. The first trademark is a camel, that is superseded by an elephant in 1897/98.

The success story

Margarete Steiff already employs ten seamstresses on the premises and another 30 ladies working in their own homes in 1897. The products are exhibited for the first time

Fig. 16 left: Company premises in 1903.

Fig. 17 top: The first business establishment in Giengen.

at the Spring Trade Fair in Leipzig, where she is accompanied by her nephew Richard Steiff. Having grown up with the felt business of their aunt, other sons of Fritz Steiff take over leading positions within the company in the years to come: Paul and Franz (1898), Otto (1902), Hugo (1906) and, finally, Ernst (1927). A packing shop is added to the existing building in 1899. Agencies are established in London, Florence and Amsterdam. More than 200 people are already working for the toy factory in 1902, the year in which Richard Steiff invents the jointed bears. A new building made of steel and glass is planned and subsequently built during the following year. Two additional buildings of the same style follow not long afterwards. The "Button in Ear" invented by Franz Steiff is attached to every Steiff animal from November 1st, 1904, onwards. The words "Knopf im Ohr" [German for "Button in Ear"] are registered as a trademark and are therefore protected by law. In 1905, the number of people employed on the premises has grown to 400 and there are 1800 ladies working for the company at home. The felt toy factory changed its name from "Filzspielwarenfabrik" to "Margarete Steiff GmbH" on June 30th, 1906. Almost a million bears are produced in 1907, the "year of the bear". Margarete Steiff begins to write her memoirs in July 1908. She then dies of pneumonia on May 9th, 1909, at the age of 62.

Fig. 20: Bear costume
made of mohair plush.

LOOKING FOR A SUITABLE MATERIAL

There is one crucial ingredient still missing, however, before Richard Steiff's idea can be realised: the right material has still to be found. It must have a natural appearance, be cuddly soft and smooth, but must also be hard-wearing.

The materials used up to this time, such as felt, short-pile plush or so-called coat plush are not really suitable, and the velvet used from 1899 onwards does not fulfil the criteria either.

An initial reference to a soft fabric with longer pile is found in 1901. Given the designation fine or glacé plush, it was initially only offered for the polar bears and brown bears on wheels, that were 50 cm tall.

There is no doubt that the fine plush referred to here is the first use of high-quality mohair plush for a regular article in the Steiff product range. In 1901, this material was manufactured by Reinhard Schulte, a Duisburg-based company that is still one of the plush suppliers to Margarete Steiff GmbH in the 21st century.

The fabrication process for this type of material involves weaving angora goat hair into a support fabric made of cotton.

Mohair plush is made with different lengths of pile and its natural properties and the various dying techniques that may be used make it an ideal solution for the realisation of Richard Steiff's plans.

The first bear costumes were also made of mohair plush. Initially, it was just human beings who were transformed into "moving Teddy bears" when they dressed up in these brown fur costumes, but that was soon to change ...

Fig. 21: Display board –
Development of mohair plush.

Fig. 18 left: Brown bear on
wheels made of mohair plush.
Fig. 19 underneath: A live bear –
model for Richard Steiff.

The Jointed Bear is Born

... PAVING THE WAY FOR THE FIRST
CAUTIOUS STEPS ALONG THE ROAD TO
WORLDWIDE SUCCESS.

Fig. 22: Two specimens of Bear
55PB pose for the 1903/04
catalogue of new articles.

Once all of the conditions required for production of the jointed bear are fulfilled, it's not long before the first presentable animal samples with jointed limbs and turning heads are created in Richard Steiff's workshop.

The very first animals to emerge are a monkey and a bear. These are given the designations "Aff 60PB" (for the monkey) and "Bär 55PB" (for the bear) in accordance with the article nomenclature used at the time. "P" stands for plush, "B" for beweglich, which is German for movable, and the numbers "60" and "55" indicate their respective sizes in centimetres. The animals are measured standing up, i.e. with the legs extended.

Paul Steiff, one of Richard's brothers and another of Margarete Steiff's nephews, is in America at this time. After joining the company in 1898, he is primarily responsible for management of the design and testing department. However, Paul's main reason for visiting America is to promote sales of Steiff animals on the other side of the Atlantic.

The American market is of prime importance. Large cities with over a million inhabitants, such as New York, Chicago or Philadelphia, for example, offer tremendous sales potential. Business is booming there and it's only a few years since America freed itself from its isolation to exert a decisive influence on global trading with its "open-door policy". One of the people responsible for this policy is the American President who has been in office since 1901: Theodore Roosevelt. And the No. 1 man in the United States is about to play an important role in our history for the second time ...

Fig. 24: Theodore Roosevelt

Paul Steiff – The man

Paul Steiff, Richards elder brother, was born on February 19th, 1876, the eldest son of Margarete Steiff's brother Fritz and his wife, Anna.

Having completed his apprenticeship as a draughtsman, Paul Steiff studied art in Stuttgart for five terms before starting to work for his aunt's company in 1898. The publication issued to celebrate the firm's 50th jubilee in 1930 describes his duties as "pattern making, i.e. duplicating, scaling down,

scaling up, preparing for series production". Many new Steiff products are created according to his designs. Paul Steiff was particularly interested in animal noises and he devoted himself to developing and perfecting the most diverse voices for the animals.

His painstakingly noted records and comments enable us to understand many correlations and occurrences that took place during the first half of the 20th century today. More of his sketchbooks and written documents from that time, in particular, have been preserved in the Steiff archives than from anyone else.

Paul worked for the felt toy factory in America for nearly two years at the beginning of the 20th century and presented the first jointed bear created by Richard Steiff there at the beginning of 1903.

He returned to Germany soon afterwards and spent the rest of his working life in the Giengen factory. Paul wrote the following lines on October 25th, 1945, at the age of 69: "I have lived through strange times. 2 world wars & the last one lost, it is impossible for us to imagine what terrible consequences this will have. Work offers us the only means of forgetting these horrors for a while." Paul Steiff dies in 1954.

Fig. 23

Fig. 25: Illustration from the 1903/04

catalogue of new articles.

THE FIRST JOURNEY ACROSS THE ATLANTIC

Documents in the Steiff archives prove that a consignment of five crates containing a total of more than 4000 Steiff animals were loaded for shipment to America at the end of 1902/beginning of 1903. They were shipped by Louis Delius & Co. of Bremen on board the "S.S. Hannover of the North German Lloyd". As shown by the documents, crates 1 to 3 contained articles ordered by American customers, while crates 4 and 5 contained samples and a small stock of articles for Paul Steiff.

The consignment arrived in America some time at the beginning of 1903, certainly before March 28th, because this was the date on which a receipt for returned merchandise from this delivery was signed by Paul Steiff. The consignment included one of the first movable bears, the 55PB.

Paul Steiff's efforts to sell the articles in America did not achieve the desired results, however. This is indicated by the hand-written note that he drew up a year later, referring to himself in the third person:

Figs. 26-27: Extracts from the complete list of items in the consignment of five crates containing a total of more than 4000 Steiff animals shipped to America. All of the crate numbers are given in this list.
The contents of crate 3945 (No. 5) also include the Bear 55PB – he appears on the list for this box.

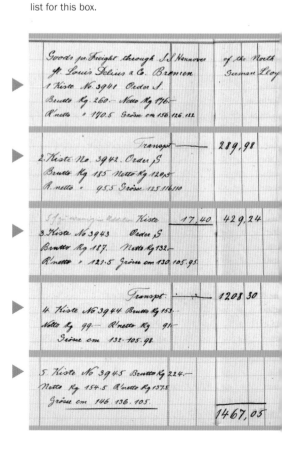

Fortlaufende Nr.	Name bezw. Firma des Anmeldenden.	Tag und Stunde der Anmeldung.	Bezeichnung des angemeldeten Musters oder Modells.	Angabe: ob das Muster für Flächenerzeugnisse oder für plastische Erzeugnisse bestimmt ist.	Schutzfrist.	Verlängerung der Schutzfrist.
1.	2.	3.	4.	5.	6.	7.

(handwritten design register entries)

"... in an effort to sell the company's toys ... he spent approximately 1 year on the other side of the Atlantic Ocean, in Connecticut & New York, where he endeavoured to do so, but met with great resistance & was therefore compelled to give up any further attempts as our toys were too expensive for the Americans, even in those days". Paul Steiff actually makes a specific reference to the first jointed bear in the next sentence: "... even the newly introduced plush Teddy bear, which was furthermore considered to be too big & heavy & hard to be suitable as a toy animal for children & was therefore criticised & did not sell, a situation that forced P. Steiff to comply with these wishes in Europe & leave the country of America".

Fig. 28: Extract from the design register dated July 13th, 1903 – a copy in Latin script can be found in the appendix on page 176.

Fig. 29: Colour panel on the front page of the 1901 Steiff Catalogue.

LEIPZIG SPRING TRADE FAIR IN 1903 & APPLICATION FOR PROTECTION OF A REGISTERED DESIGN

The Bear 55PB must have been presented to the public in Germany for the first time at the Leipzig Spring Trade Fair in 1903. Nonetheless, authentic documents relating to the trade fair that almost certainly led to the final breakthrough for Richard Steiff's invention, have not been discovered up to now. It was not until 1955, just in time for the 75th company jubilee of Margarete Steiff GmbH, that an order from America was mentioned, one that has since been quoted numerous times. According to this source of information, a buyer from the American company Geo. Borgfeldt & Co. placed an order for 3000 of the 55PB bears on the last day of the trade fair.

Fig. 32: The application for protection of a registered design dated August 7th, 1902 – a copy in Latin script can be found in the appendix on page 178.

Fig. 30: This detail from the catalogue of new articles in 1903/04 shows a considerably touched-up Bear 55PB in the company of the Monkey 60PB.

Regardless of whatever actually happened in Leipzig or anywhere else in the world on that day, this order for 3000 Steiff Teddies is rather a mystery, particularly as there are no known records of any shipment to America. Neither has any evidence been found in America to support the theory that these articles were imported.

The story of the wedding that was attended by Theodore Roosevelt, where Steiff bears were used as table decorations, also dates back to the 1950s. This story, which has now become a well-known wonderful fairytale, will be discussed at greater length in the chapter about how Teddy got his name.

What is indisputable and can be proved without any shadow of doubt, however, is that applications for protection of registered designs were recorded for the Steiff Bear 55PB and the Monkey 60PB at Heidenheim district court as early as July 13th, 1903. "Margarete Steiff – Erste Spielwarenfabrik Deutschlands" [first toy factory in Germany] as the Margarete Steiff GmbH of today is known at the time, only submits applications for protection of registered designs at irregular intervals.

The application dated July 13th, 1903 was preceded by an application dated August 7th, 1902. That one applies to five felt dolls: two policemen, a football player, a black football player and a frog oarsman. These dolls have jointed arms and legs and are therefore mentioned again below.

The intervals between the various applications for protection of registered designs and the joints used in the felt dolls are further indications in favour of the theory

Fig. 31: Everyone loves Teddy – irrespective of age.

fende	Name bezw. Firma des Anmeldenden.	Tag und Stunde der Anmeldung.	Bezeichnung des angemeldeten Musters oder Modells.	Angabe: ob das Muster für Flächenerzeugnisse oder für plastische Erzeugnisse bestimmt ist.	Schuhfrist.	Verlängerung der Schuhfrist.
	2.	3.	4.	5.	6.	7.
	Margarete Steiff, Filzspiel- werenfabrik in Gien- hans a Bry	*3. März 1902 nachmittts 6 Uhr*	*ein ausspielgelter Perhats, enthaltend 8 verschiedene, bemalte u nicht verschiedenen Waffen bekleidete Spielpuppen in Gie Gestalt von Menschen Tieren. Fabrikmarke: Polier 70 35 77, « 70 50 87, Sportkellner 70 75 85, Magnus 70 35 82. Röhrchen (Steiff) 70 75 85.*	*plastische Erzeugnisse.*	*3 Jahre*	
2)		*3. Februar 1905*	*verzeichnet*	–		*3 Jahre*

that the first jointed bear was developed and created in 1902.

To make one thing clear right from the start: there is not a single known survivor from Richard Steiff's first series of the Bear 55PB around today.

Photographic evidence from that time is also extremely rare. The most well-known illustration is taken from the 1903/04 catalogue of new articles. It shows the Bear 55PB with the Monkey 60PB. The original illustration used for printing has been preserved in the Steiff archives. It has, however, been touched up to such an extent that it no longer constitutes a reliable record of the first movable bear's actual appearance. Neither does it provide any information concerning his insides, particularly with respect to the way in which the moving limbs and turning head were connected to the body.

Nonetheless, it is this illustration from the catalogue of new articles that provides the crucial clue to solving the mystery surrounding the construction of the first jointed bear.

Fig. 33: Illustration of the jointed felt dolls of 1902.

Forefather of the Teddy Bear

WHAT DID HE LOOK LIKE, THE VERY

FIRST JOINTED BEAR?

ON THE TRAIL OF THE SECRETS

SURROUNDING THE CONSTRUCTION

AND APPEARANCE OF THE 55PB ...

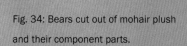

Fig. 34: Bears cut out of mohair plush
and their component parts.

Fig. 35: The motto adopted by Margarete Steiff for the production of toys as early as 1892.

The name of the key that solves the mystery of what goes on inside the Teddy is "Aff 60PB", the monkey.

As already mentioned above, the Bear 55PB and Monkey 60PB that appeared together in the 1903/04 catalogue of new articles were also registered together as protected designs. As luck would have it, at least the monkey that was registered at Heidenheim district court with the bear on July 13th, 1903, has fortunately been preserved in the Steiff archive. Even the tag that identifies him as No. 8 for the application is still attached to his body.

The solution to the mystery was at least near at hand. The next question was how best to find out what was going on inside the monkey.

It goes without saying that this had to be done without damaging such a valuable specimen. Conventional X-ray techniques that could give an insight into a Steiff animal's "insides" do not offer a suitable means of making strong-thread jointing or cord connections visible as they are only capable of clearly showing high-density materials, such as bone or metal. Although this would have been adequate to indicate the metal joints of the next generation of bears, the 28PB, it is unsuitable for the current application.

Ultrasonic equipment of the type also used for diagnosis of internal organs require application of a gel to act as a medium between the body under examination and the recording unit in order to work effectively. This requirement therefore eliminates the possibility of such a technique being used to investigate a Steiff animal with mohair fur.

The desired results are finally achieved with state-of-the-art X-ray technology of the type used to check luggage at airports. The following X-ray images were produced by an HS 6040 I device (HS stands for High Scan) manufactured by Heimann Systems GmbH.

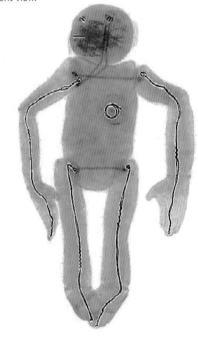

Fig. 36: X-ray image of the Monkey 60PB – front view.

X-RAYS SHOW WHAT HE'S MADE OF

100 years have now passed since Richard Steiff created the jointed Teddy bear ... and we are now getting close to solving the mystery surrounding his construction and appearance ...

The X-ray image has been post-processed, dying the cord connections red to show them more clearly. Both arms and legs are evidently joined to one another by thick cords that run through the body of the monkey. The ends of each cord are knotted several times in the arms and legs.

Fig. 37: Monkey 60PB
from the Steiff archive.

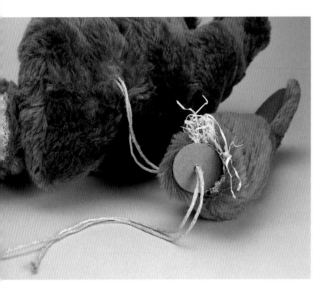

Fig. 38 Detail: The partially filled arm is attached to the body.

Cardboard disks are used to secure the knots and prevent them from tearing through the fabric when the arms and legs are moved. This means that each individual limb can be rotated about its knot without moving the cord.

The manufacturing process involves the following steps: the arms and legs are only packed with wood shavings until they are three-quarters full, the cord that runs through the body is then led into the limb, pulled tight and is subsequently knotted firmly on the inside of the disk. The arms and legs can then be filled completely and closed with a hand-stitched seam.

These cardboard disks are only fitted in the arms and legs, not in the main body of the animal, because additional disks inside the body would not perform any useful purpose with this method of fastening.

The Monkey 60PB was produced at the same time as the Bear 55PB, which implies that the make-up of the first jointed bear was very probably the same, with a similar type of internal construction.

This means that the frequently voiced theory, which explains the lack of any surviving first-generation jointed bears by suggesting that their arms and legs were torn away from their bodies after being turned just a few times, seems extremely unlikely. Margarete Steiff's quality requirements would certainly not have permitted the presentation of a product like this to potential customers, even as a sample. The joining method described above was also employed for the felt dolls that were registered as protected designs in 1902. In this case, however, the cords are knotted on the outside of each limb. Small disks are also used for this technique, whereby these are made of leather and are fitted between the knot and the felt.

Being much lighter than the plush animals, the dolls permit this simple type of fastening as there is less likelihood that the arms or legs will be torn off or pulled away. Although the knots are tied on the outside of each limb, they are cleverly concealed under the felt clothing and are therefore virtually invisible.

The twin wires that appear as black lines running through the arms and legs on the X-ray image are not attached to the cords. This is because any fixed connec-

Fig. 39 Detail: Knot tied outside for the felt dolls.

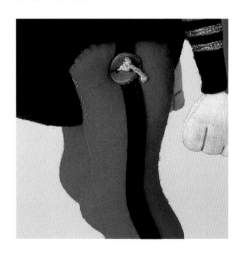

Fig. 40: British bobbies –
early felt dolls.

tions between cord and limbs would inevitably cause the cord to break or the cardboard disk to tear after just a few turns and lead to the loss of an arm or leg.

The wires are primarily used to stabilise the arms and legs, which are particularly long in the case of the monkey. Apart from this, they also offer a means of holding the arms and legs in fixed positions – but only to the extent permitted by the very restricted pliability of the used materials.

The arms of the first models of the Bear 55PB were also very long, so it is reasonable to suppose that they also had these wires fitted in them.

Apart from the monkey preserved in the Steiff archive, however, no other examples of any bears or monkeys with wire reinforcements in arms or legs have come to light up to now. This implies that they were only used in the first prototype specimens.

The way in which the head is attached to the body is interesting and baffling at the same time. The X-ray image showing a side view of the Monkey 60PB clearly shows the two metal rings from the shoe-button eyes. The two lengths of cord used to secure the eyes to the head are attached to these.

The relatively fine cords are normally drawn through to the undersurface at the back of the head and knotted on the outside to ensure that the eyes are fitted securely. This was the usual method of securing shoe-button eyes up to the beginning of the 1920s and was even used as late as the 1960s for glass eyes.

The method used for the Monkey 60PB is completely different. The two cords were brought together and knotted at the back of the head, but inside it. Two other, considerably thicker cords are attached to this knot and run through the head to the neck by the shortest possible route. They leave the head at this point and are drawn back into the neck of the stuffed body with a long needle (cf. Fig. 44).

Fig. 41: The knot holding head and body together is virtually invisible.

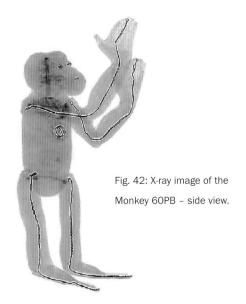

Fig. 42: X-ray image of the Monkey 60PB – side view.

Fig. 43 top: X-ray image showing the cord connections between head and body coloured red.

Fig. 44 left: The cords secured in the head are drawn into the body.

Fig. 45: Steiff monkeys enjoying a lesson in PE.

The wood-shaving packer then leads the needle with the two cords out of the body again, just below the location of the cord joint for the monkey's right arm. The cords are tensioned and knotted firmly on the outside. This produces a permanent connection between head and body, whereby the knot is almost invisible as it is hidden between the arm and the body (cf. Fig. 41 on page 32).

A similar procedure to that used for the arms and legs must be adopted for the head. The shoe-button eyes are drawn into the head when about half of the wood-shaving filling has been packed into it and the cords are knotted together inside the back of the head. The two thicker cords are tied to this knot and are then drawn through the middle of the head to connect it to the body. The rest of the stuffing is then packed into the head which is then closed with a hand-stitched seam in the vicinity of the join.

Incidentally, this method of securing the head to the body cannot be mastered by muscle-power alone. Even strapping men who still stuff the wood shavings into the articles at Margarete Steiff GmbH today have to admit defeat after many courageous attempts. A tensioning facility had to be developed and built especially for this purpose in order to achieve a secure connection between head and body.

Fig. 46: Steiff also produced jointed camels from 1908 onwards.

Fig. 47: A jointed cat was added to the Steiff product range as early as 1904.

Fig. 48: One of the few photographs of the Bear 55PB still in existence. The original black-and-white photograph was coloured according to the results of the grey-scale analysis.

Fig. 49: The cone nose, the pronounced hump and the long arms and legs are evidence of this Teddy bear's early manufacture.

A BROWN BEAR IN BLACK AND WHITE: WHAT THE 55PB LOOKED LIKE

The colouring is another one of the mysteries surrounding the appearance of the Bear 55PB because the few photographs that have survived the passage of time are black and white, of course.

Modern computer technology has proved to be very useful in this respect too: a technique referred to as grey-scale analysis enables the conversion of existing black-and-white photographs into colour images. The result is as simple as it is logical – the colour of the first jointed bear corresponds to the natural colour of a brown bear.

Even if there are no examples of the first jointed Bear 55PB still in existence today, all of the knowledge regarding his construction and appearance that has been acquired and recounted up to now is exclusively based on verifiable facts. Monkey 60PB lives in the Steiff archive along with the early felt dolls, several examples of the Bear 35PB and all of the written and photographic documents dating back to the early years that has been used here.

35

55PB's
IV. Descendants

THE TECHNIQUES
USED TO JOIN THE
TEDDY TOGETHER ARE
OPTIMISED, HIS APPEAR-
ANCE CHANGES AND,
QUITE INCIDENTAL-
LY, WE DISCOVER
AS YET UNDIS-
CLOSED
SECRETS CON-
CERNING
BEAR 55PB ...

FROM BEAR ...

Fig. 50:
Bear 35PB

... TO "BÄRLE"

Fig. 51:
"Bärle 5328"

Fig. 52:

The Pinscher 35PB –

a certain similarity with a

cuddly bear cannot be

denied.

Although there is no known documentary evidence of the actual production figures for 1903 to 1905, this gap can be closed to a great extent with reference to catalogues that have been preserved over the years, entries in the register of protected designs and early bears that have survived the passage of time. That is of great significance as far as the history of our current Teddy bear is concerned and very important to the many Steiff collectors all over the world.

The anniversary publication issued to celebrate the company's 50th jubilee in 1930, for example, contains one specific item of information from this early period: a total of 12,000 bears were manufactured during 1904. There are, however, no details that indicate how this figure was distributed over the various models. The first remaining record of this type of information dates back to 1906 and takes the form of complete order and production lists for each year (refer to page 58).

The first Steiff catalogue in 1904 is issued on February 1st – just in time for the Leipzig Trade Fair held between 7th and 12th March – and the offered range of jointed animals comprises a bear, the Bear 55PB, the familiar Monkey 60PB, a Monkey 43PB, a different-sized monkey that was already included in the product spectrum in 1903, and a Pinscher 35PB has been added to the Steiff collection to replace the Pinscher 55PB which appeared in the 1903/04 catalogue of new articles. This pinscher was only available until 1906 and he does not appear in any catalogue or on any of the many photographic plates dating back to this time that are preserved in the Steiff archives.

He wasn't registered as a protected design either. 70 of these animals were produced in 1906, which implies that the model was only manufactured in very small numbers. As far as we know,

Fig. 53: Design copyright registration dated March 5th, 1904 – a copy in Latin script can be found in the appendix on page 180.

Fortlaufende Nr.	Name bezw. Firma des Anmeldenden.	Tag und Stunde der Anmeldung.	Bezeichnung des angemeldeten Musters oder Modells.	Angabe: ob das Muster für Flächenerzeugnisse oder für plastische Erzeugnisse bestimmt ist.	Schutzfrist.	Verlängerung der Schutzfrist.
1.	2.	3.	4.	5.	6.	7.
14.		5. März 1904				

Fig. 54: Even standing up, the
Pinscher 35PB resembles a bear
more than a dog.

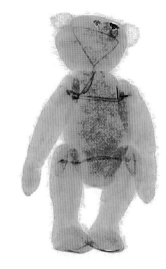

there is only one surviving pinscher and he now lives in the doll's house museum ("Puppenhausmuseum") in Basle. Fairly graceful in real life, the toy animal bears very little resemblance to a live pinscher. Maybe that is why so few of them were produced ...

Bear 35PB was registered as a protected design at Heidenheim court as early as March 5th, 1904 (refer to Fig. 53 on page 38), just two days before the Leipzig Trade Fair. That means that, even if he did not appear in the 1904 trade fair catalogue, he was already in existence at the time of the trade fair and could be presented to the visitors in Leipzig.

Entered under serial number 9, two other types of animal were registered at the same time. "Esl 43PB" (a donkey) and "Ele 35PB" (an elephant). Both donkey and elephant were produced as jointed versions for the very first time – two new members of the family of toy animals with movable limbs.

Fig. 55: X-ray photograph of the Bear 35PB.

BEAR 55PB AND BEAR 35PB: CLOSE RELATIVES?

To find out whether the 35PB is closely related to his predecessor, Bear 55PB, let us first take a look at his X-ray photograph: with the cord connections (marked in red) and the cardboard disks, it is obvious that the limbs are joined to the body in the same manner as described in detail for the Monkey 60PB (refer to Chapter III). The head is also secured in exactly the same way, apart from a few minor differences in the routing of the cord inside the head. Wires are no longer used in the arms and legs of Bear 35PB. However, as shown by an analysis of the X-ray photograph of Monkey 60PB, these do not serve any purpose as far as securing the limbs is concerned.

Fig. 56: Teddy also enjoys his freedom of movement in a bathing suit.

Fig. 57: These two
Teddy ladies take a
leisurely stroll.

Fig. 58: A real Teddy
mother is always there for
her offspring.

Monkey 60PB is created at around the same time as the 55PB. And the same technique is still used to secure the arms and legs of Bear 35PB more than a year later. Can the monkey help to solve the mystery surrounding the very first jointed bear ever produced, the prototype that has remained lost without trace up to the present day?

He certainly can: the monkey again turns out to be the critical piece in the jigsaw puzzle of the search for detailed information concerning the 55PB. The monkey is first weighed and measured. Standing up, he is 57 cm tall and he weighs 805 g.

The photograph showing Monkey 60PB and Bear 55PB standing next to one another from the 1903/04 catalogue of new articles clearly indicates that the monkey is taller than the bear. Considering their sizes in relation to one another, it would appear that Bear 55PB was actually around 52 cm tall (plus or minus 1 cm).

The same weighing and measuring procedure is carried out on Bear 35PB – with baffling results. Assuming a maximum deviation of just 2 cm, he would appear to be the same size as the 55PB! This is because, measured standing up, the 35PB is actually 50 cm tall and weighs 890 g.

The next stage involves comparing weights, but neither the 1903 catalogue of new articles nor the 1904 trade fair catalogue contain any relevant details. The first catalogue to offer such information dates back to 1905: Monkey 60PPB weighs 990 g and Bear 35PB weighs 1050 g. (Incidentally, the jointed monkey was not only available in mohair, but also as a coat plush version. The jointed monkey made of coat plush had already been given the designation 'PB' – 'P' for 'plush' and 'B' for 'beweglich' (German for movable), so another 'P' was added to the designation for the mohair monkey, which became known as 'PPB'. The bear with the 'PB' designation was only ever made of mohair, however, which meant that the 'PB' designation for the bear had the same meaning as the 'PPB' designation for the monkey. The extract from the 1905 Steiff catalogue shown on the right-hand side illustrates this not altogether unambiguous system of designations.)

The actual weight of the 57 cm-tall monkey differs from that quoted in the catalogue by 185 g. Amounting to less than 20%, this

Fig. 59: Extract from the 1905
Steiff price list.

ENGROS-PREISLISTE
(Nachdruck verboten.) (15. 8.) **1905.**

Bisherige Bezeichnung	Stück-gewicht Kilo	Nummer	Stück M. Pf.	Bisherige Bezeichnung	Stück-gewicht Kilo	Nummer	Stück M. Pf.
Affe. (10)				**Bär.** (12)			
(aufwartend)				(stehend)			
Aff 8 G*	0.02	4108	-. 33	Bär 8 G	0.04	1208,0	-. 33
Aff 14 G*	0.07	4114	-. 60	Bär 14 G	0.07	1214,0	-. 60
Aff 17 G*	0.09	4117	-. 80	Bär 17	0.18	1217	1.50
Aff 17 G* Fr. . .	0.09	4117,6	1.20	Bär 22	0.66	1222	2.75
Aff 22 G	0.14	4122	1.50	Bär 28	1.12	1228	4.25
(beweglich)				Bär 35	1.9	1235	6. —
Aff 28 Clon . . .	0.11	5128	1.50	Bär 43	3.6	1243	8. —
Aff 35 Clon . . .	0.15	5135	1.75	Bär 50	5.00	1250	12. —
Aff 43 Clon . . .	0.3	5143	2.65	Bär 60	8.2	1260	15. —
Aff 50 Clon . . .	0.41	5150	3.50	Bär 99	19.7	1299	35. —
Aff 60 Clon . . .	0.66	5160	4.40	Bär 17 fein . . .	0.3	1317	2.50
Aff 80 Clon . . .	1.2	5180	7.15	Bär 22 fein . . .	0.66	1322	4. —
Aff 100 Clon . . .	3.0	5199	12. —	Bär 28 fein . . .	1.08	1328	6.15
Aff 35 PB	0,22	5235	1.50	Bär 35 fein . . .	1.7	1335	9. —
Aff 43 PB	0.35	5243	1.90	Bär 43 fein . . .	3.2	1343	12.50
Aff 35 PPB . . .	0.22	5335	2.50	Bär 50 fein . . .	4.4	1350	17.50
Aff 43 PPB . . .	0.37	5343	3.25	Bär 60 fein . . .	7.28	1360	24. —
Aff 50 PPB . . .	0.57	5350	4. —	Bär 8 Mo R* . .	0.04	1408,0	—. 70
Aff 60 PPB . . .	0.99	5360	6.40	(tanzend)			
Aff 70 PPB . . .	1.25	5370	9. —	Bär 17 Tanz* . .	0.09	4217	-. 65
Aff 80 PPB . . .	1.9	5380	10.50	Bär 70 Tanz . .	8.6	4270	9.80
Aff 90 PPB . . .	3.00	5390	14. —	(beweglich)			
Aff 120 PPB . . .	6.15	53120	22.50	Bärle 17 PAB .	0.09	5317,1	1.60
				Bärle 22 PAB .	0.17	5322,1	2.50
Apfel, Ballon, Birne, Blumen siehe **Rassel (83).**				Bärle 28 PB .	0.58	5328	5. —
				Bärle 28 PAB .	0.85	5328,1	5. —
				Bärle 35 PB .	1.05	5335	8. —
				Bärle 35 PAB .	0.61	5335,1	8. —
				Bärle 43 PAB .	0.98	5343,1	12. —
				Bärle 50 PAB .	1.88	5350,1	14. —
				Bärle 80 PAB .	5.4	5380,1	30. —

Fig. 60: Monkey 60PB and Bear 35PB –
there is no denying the correspondence
with the photograph from the 1903 catalogue. Bear 35PB has taken the place
of his predecessor Bear 55PB in this
photograph. Refer to Fig. 30 on page
24 for the original illustration.

Fig. 61: Jointed Steiff animals and dolls
demonstrate their movability.

Fig. 62: Bear 28PB.

deviation corresponds to a number of weighing results obtained for other items from this time. To a certain extent, it can be attributed to a weight loss caused by the excelsior drying out and the catalogues frequently also quoted the tare weights (toy animal with packaging).

The difference in weight for Bear 35PB amounts to as little as 160 g, which corresponds to a deviation of just 15% from the original weight. Relatively small for products dating back to that time, the deviations in size and weight, which are quite normal and well within the tolerance limits, certainly imply that the weight quoted for Bear 35PB could well be similar to that of the 55PB. The fact that, in 1905 the article designation for the monkey still indicates its size when standing whereas the article number for the bear reflects its height in a sitting position, must also be taken into consideration.

A close relationship between the two bears – the 55 and 35PB – is also implied by their respective prices. The 1903 catalogue of new articles, the 1904 trade fair catalogue and the wholesale price list from 1905 quote the following prices: the Monkey 60PB costs 6 marks in 1903 and 1904, with just a slight price increase in 1905, i.e. 6.40 marks. The relationship is the same for the Monkey 43PB, priced at 3.15 marks in 1903 and 1904 and increasing to 3.25 marks in 1905. A Bear 55PB can be purchased for 8 marks in 1903 and 1904, which is exactly the same price that is quoted for the Bear 35PB in the 1905 catalogue.

"Pintscher 35PB" is also offered at the same price in the 1904 catalogue, whereas the price for "Pintscher 55PB" amounted to 7 marks in 1903. The price structure did not undergo any major changes during those two years, so it seems unlikely that the catalogues refer to two different pinschers. Here too, the different sizes imply a change in the method of measuring. In the light of this evidence, it can hardly be regarded as merely speculation to suggest that 55PB and 35PB are identical to the greatest extent possible.

In spite of many concurring factors, we still cannot assume that there were no differences whatever between the two models of bear. The most obvious difference is the colour: while the 55PB was made of brown mohair, beautiful blond mohair is used in the production of the 35PB. The coat plush that can be regarded as being an early stage of mohair plush was available in brown, white and grey at the time. The new blond colouring was used for the first time in manufacturing the jointed pinscher and Bear 35PB, both of which were made of mohair.

Fig. 63: Some jointed bears also have to wear muzzles.

Another deviation is evident on the enlarged section of the illustration of the two bears playing on page 35 shown on the right: the nose of the 55PB is reminiscent of a flat button or disk, although it could be an early version of the nose made of sealing wax that was first used in 1904. The previously produced bears on wheels already had stitched noses, however, which means that the possibility that the prototype had a stitched nose – unlike the one shown on the photograph – cannot be ruled out completely.

As there are no verifiable records of the sales figures for 1903, and not a single Bear 55PB is known to have survived up to now, it seems likely that only a very few samples were actually produced. The sales figures recorded for 1904 were therefore probably achieved with Bear 35PB and, towards the end of that year, with the 28PB.

Fig. 64: Enlarged detail
of Bear 55PB's nose.

35PB's little brother: Bear 28PB

Bear 28PB is another of Bear 55PB's descendants. Nobody seems to know the exact date of his debut in the family of movable toy animals so far. However, the utility-model patent on the internal wire fastening technique for the moving limbs that was registered on December 5th, 1904, and the application for rights to further develop this technique (using a metal rod to join the movable parts together) dated June 8th, 1905, must be regarded as being directly connected with the creation of Bear 28PB.

The patented wire fastening technique was only used in the felt dolls initially, the subsequently developed rod was adopted as standard for Bear 28PB.

With the passage of time, it becomes evident again and again that the knowledge acquired in manufacturing the felt dolls was implemented and applied – with slight changes – throughout the development of the jointed bear. Unlike the cord connections used in the 35PB, metal rods secure the head as well as the limbs of the Bear 28PB. The top end of the rod used to connect head to body is secured with a cap. In the stuffing process, the excelsior is therefore packed into the head last of all, and from the top. The bear is finally closed with a hand-stitched seam that runs from one ear to the other.

It goes without saying that the 28PB is also smaller than the Bear 35PB: made of shiny plush, the playmate measures 28 cm sitting down and 40 cm standing up. The catalogue dated August 15th, 1905, transforms the Bear 28PB that costs 5 marks into "Bärle 28PB". Like his brother, the 35PB, this is the last time that he is included in the product range.

Fig. 65: This drawing was submitted with the registration for a utility-model patent for a "toy with movable limbs that are joined together with a twin wire which has closures inside the body of the toy" at Heidenheim district court on December 5th, 1904.

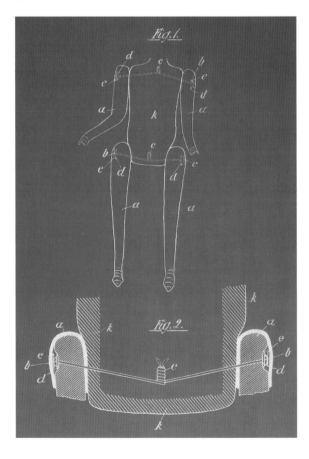

Fig. 66: The X-ray photograph
shows the metal rods securing
the limbs that were typical for
the Bear 28PB.

Fig. 67: Bear 28PB,
35PB's little brother, has a completely
innovative system securing the head
and limbs inside him.

THE MARKETING CONCEPT: THE BUTTON IN EAR

Margarete Steiff developed a brilliant marketing strategy in 1904 and announced her revolutionary idea to the public on November 1st. The 35PB is the only bear included in the Steiff collection at this time, but the 28PB will be launched onto the market in just a few weeks time. Item 19 in an information sheet that begins with the words "Hiermit ersuche ich höflichst von Nachstehendem gefl. Kenntnis zu nehmen" [I most respectfully request that attention be drawn to the following], refers to a "Trademark; (elephant with an S-shaped trunk) on a small nickel button which I shall attach to every single article, without exception, from November 1st, 1904, onwards, in the left ear. A patent on this method of attachment has been registered."

If the buttons were actually fitted on and after this precise date, all Bears 28PB must have been supplied with an elephant button right from the very beginning and only a few isolated bears manufactured at a later date would have had a blank button. Most of the 35PBs, on the other hand, did not have buttons in their ears at all because production of that bear reached its peak prior to this date. This assumption is confirmed to a great extent by the Steiff buttons in the ears of the known examples of these two models of bear in the current collectors' market.

Fig. 68: The jointed Steiff monkey – can hardly be told apart from a living monkey.

19) **Schutzmarke**; (Elefant mit S-förmigem Rüssel) befestige ich ab 1. Nov. 1904 nunmehr ausnahmslos an jedes Stück an und zwar im linken Ohr auf einem kleinen Nickelknöpfchen. Auf diese Art der Anbringung ist gesetzlicher Schutz angemeldet.

Beilage

Fig. 69: Extract from a publication dating back to 1904: announcement of the "Button in Ear".

Button, Ear Tag & Chest Tag

The so-called "elephant button" of the Steiff company heralded the introduction of the "Button in Ear" trademark in 1904. Just a year later, it is supplemented by the attachment of an ear tag bearing the relevant article data. Another mark of recognition is added in the middle of the 1920s in the form of a pendant that is attached to every Steiff animal and becomes known as the chest tag.

All three distinguishing features – button, ear tag and chest tag – have altered or been replaced by new types many times over the years. For the collector of today,

they not only provide a means of identification, but also give a fairly accurate indication of the date of an animal's creation. At the time, these trademarks were solely attached to safeguard the interests of the company – nobody even thought about future collectors, of course. Old stocks of buttons or ear tags were therefore always used up, even if new models were already available. As a result, one occasionally comes across Steiff animals with identification markings that do not agree with the information summarised below: for example, Steiff buttons that indisputably date

back to the 1930s are attached to articles that, because of the presence of a US-zone tag, were undeniably manufactured after the 2nd World War. A certain amount of experience is needed in order to give an unequivocal assessment of such special cases and this experience can only be acquired within the framework of a deep involvement in the collectors' world – if in doubt, it is always advisable to consult a specialist.

Incidentally, the button is the only distinguishing mark that was used continuously (except for the cheap articles produced

Fig. 70: Role reversal –
the monkey clown in charge
of the bear.

during the 1930s). The ear tag was not
used at all for a long time, and was not
attached to all articles until the middle of
the 1920s.
Every period had its special articles that
required different distinguishing marks by
virtue of their nature or size, of course.
Examples of these include the miniature
woollen articles, wooden toys, vehicles and
the large-scale studio animals.
The following summary contains illustra-
tions of the most important trademarks
and gives details of the periods in which
they were used.

Fig. 71:
From 1.11.1904
to 1905:
Use of the elephant
button

Fig. 72:
1905 to 1906:
Blank button, white tag
with printed article
number, the word
"geschützt" (patented) was also used occasionally.
Although the blank button was only used up to
1906, the illustrated tag was attached up to
around 1908.

Fig. 73:
1906 to 1924:
Button with the name
"Steiff" in upper-case
letters, the second "f"
in Steiff extended into a long arc, white tag with
printed article number and "Steiff Original".

THE NEW PAB SERIES IS BORN

Since its creation in 1902, advances in the jointed bear have been primarily oriented to improving the techniques used to secure its limbs and head, whereas the style remains the same. The only slight difference in its visual appearance has been brought about by the use of lighter coloured mohair. The jointed plush bear still bears a strong resemblance to the live animals on which he was modelled ...

This finally changes when a new series of Teddy bears sees the light of day on February 15th, 1905, just in time for the important Leipzig Trade Fair: the date on which a design copyright was registered for "Bärle 35PAB" at Heidenheim district court.

Button, Ear Tag & Chest Tag (Continued)

Fig. 74:
1923 to 1926:
Button as described above, white tag with printed article number, "Steiff Original geschützt" (patented) and "Germany Importé d'Allemagne".

Fig. 75:
1926 to 1934:
Button as described above, red tag with printed article number, "Steiff Original geschützt" (patented) and "Made in Germany".

Fig. 76:
1934 to 1943:
Button as described above, yellow tag with the same printed information as the red tag, "Steiff Original geschützt", abbreviated to "Steiff Orig. gesch." in some cases.

Fig. 77:
1936 to 1950:
Button with the arc from the second "f" in Steiff shortened, tag as described above.

Fig. 78:
1946 to 1950:
Blank button, sometimes painted blue, light yellow or white tag with printed "Steiff Original geschützt" (patented) and "Made in Germany".

Fig. 79:
1947 to 1952:
Button with the name "Steiff" in large uppercase letters, second "f" not extended, tag as described above.

Fig. 80:
1947 to 1953:
US-zone tag, usually sewn into a seam on the right arm or leg – certificate of origin prescribed after the 2nd World War.

Fig. 81:
1952 to 1969:
Button with Steiff name in script, yellow tag with printed article number, the Steiff name in script – like the button – and various other alternatives: "Steiff Original" or "Original Steiff", "Made in Germany" and "Preis – Price", sometimes with information about the materials on the reverse side from 1950 onwards.

Fig. 82:
1969 to 1978:
"Lentil" button, compression rivet with the Steiff name stamped onto it, yellow tag with printed article number, "Original Steiff" and "Made in Germany".

Fig. 83:
A brass button is used **from 1978** onwards, the appearance of the tag changes several times as importance is also attached to finding a means of distinguishing collectors' articles from 1980.

Fig. 84: The new model of jointed bear is simply irresistible.

Richard Steiff's unceasing efforts to further develop his bears result in a new PAB series – 'P' for plush, 'A' for angescheibt (German for disk-jointed) and 'B' for beweglich (German for movable) – which is completely different from the previous models. The head and limbs are each secured to the body with two disks, made of cardboard or metal, that are fastened together with a split-pin. One disk is fitted in the body and the other one is in the head or limb to be secured. The two disks are joined together with a metal split-pin, offering a means of fastening arms, legs and the head to the bear's body.

The new fastening technique does not require the body to be packed as tightly as before, which means that a softer packing material can be used from now on, in this case a mixture of excelsior and kapok (fibre covering the seeds of a species of silk-cotton tree). This reduces the weight of the bear considerably – a very welcome development for the children who play with the toy bear! With a weight reduction of 440 g, "Bärle 35PAB" is more than 40% lighter than the 35PB, his predecessor of the same size.

The new series also involves substantial changes in the bear's appearance. There is no better way to describe the appearance of Richard Steiff's new creation than the term "Bärenpuppe" (bear doll) used in the 1930 jubilee publication: the arms are shorter and the hump is not as pronounced, and the bear has a friendly expression

Fig. 85: Richard Steiff's famous grey bear has lost none of his attraction and admirers of all ages still succumb to his fascinating power.

Button, Ear Tag & Chest Tag (Continued)

Pendants or chest tags were not always attached to all Steiff animals until toy production started up again after the 2nd World War. Before that, they were usually attached to animals that had names, such as "Bully" the dog or "Fluffy" the cat.

There were no pendants for Teddy bears until after 1949. Much sought-after among today's collectors, these Steiff features were previously only attached to special models of jointed bears, e.g. "Dicky", "Petsy", "Teddy-clown", "Music Teddy" or "Teddy Baby".

Fig. 86:
1926 to 1928:
Pendant in various sizes, white with metal surround, printed black lettering.

Fig. 87:
1928 to 1952:
Pendant with red edging, angular yellow bear's head, pale pink inner section, printed red lettering.

Fig. 88:
1952 to 1953:
Pendant as described above, bear's head more rounded, pale yellow inner section, printed red lettering.

Fig. 89:
1953 to 1972:
Pendant as described above, bear's head completely rounded, pale yellow inner section, printed blue lettering.

Fig. 90:
From 1972 onwards:
Round pendant, divided into two halves, one red and one yellow, lettering in each half printed in the other colour. Other versions of pendant also used to identify collector's items and articles produced on behalf of industrial concerns.

Fig. 91: Richard Steiff with his "Bärle". With his completely new visual and technical design, this is the first animal to be equipped with disk-type arm and leg joints and his appearance is very similar to that of the Teddy bear that we all know and love today.

on his face. The generally more rounded contours have turned what used to be a wild bear into a proper toy animal, an adorable, huggable, cuddly bear.

Apart from the "Bärle 35PAB" registered with the court and measuring 35 cm sitting down, the 1905 catalogue also offers bears in the following sizes (also measured in a sitting position): 17, 22, 28, 43, 50 and 80 cm. All models are available in light brown, dark brown and white.

Another bear has become a very important figure in connection with the re-creation of "Bärle": the 32 cm grey bear developed by Richard Steiff. He has fortunately been preserved in the Steiff archive – where Mrs. Dehlinger, Richard's mother-in-law brought him in 1942. The bear owes his worldwide fame to the photograph that shows him with Richard Steiff, which has also survived the passage of time. This bear has been known as the Richard Steiff Bear ever since. He has a growler, four claws stitched onto each front and rear paw and he weighs 287 g.

Growlers were not invented until 1908, which means that the Richard Steiff Bear could not have been produced before 1908. He was probably a design sample for advertising purposes and trade fairs as Teddy bears made of grey mohair were never

Fig. 92: The Richard Steiff Bear is now on display in the Steiff Museum.

Steiff's Article Numbering System from 1905

The launching of the "Bärle PAB" in 1905 also heralds the implementation of Steiff's new article numbering system that will not be superseded by a more modern method until 1968. A "eloquent" sequence of numbers enables the classification and unequivocal identification of the numerous articles. The article numbers are used in the Steiff catalogues and also appear on the ear tags of every Steiff product.

Each numeral in the four-digit article number has a separate meaning and can be used to describe the material and nature of the respective article. The new article number for "Bärle 35PAB" is "5335,1". The meaning of this number is explained in the following section:

The first "5" (thousands digit) indicates the position or nature of the bear: the bear in our example is "jointed". The second digit (hundreds) describes the material of which he is made: this article is made of mohair ("3"). The third and fourth digits (tens and ones) indicate the size of the article in cm ("35"). Jointed bears are always measured sitting down, which means that our "Bärle" measures 35 cm in a sitting position.

The numbers and letters after the comma usually stand for outfitting details. The "1" in our example means that "Bärle" is a soft-filled animal. The digit after the comma is occasionally also used to distinguish between differently dressed versions of a particular animal. The Steiff product

range in the 1930s included a clothed bear named "Puppbär" (Bear Doll), for example, that was available in eleven different versions, numbered from 1 to 11. If there is no comma in an article number, such letters as br, c, g or w may be used to differentiate between brown, caramel, gold or white bears or animals. The letters M and B distinguish the girls or maids (M) from the boys (B).

Steiff adds another two digits, or three in exceptional cases, in front of the article number to avoid confusion between different types of animals. After all, the article number described above could also apply to a jointed, soft-filled elephant measuring 35 cm that is made of mohair. Referred to

Fig. 93: Wonderful scenes can also be composed with Teddy bears.

as serial numbers, "12" is used for bears and "20" is used for elephants. The serial number is rarely printed on the ear tag, but it always appears in the catalogues.

Article numbers on Steiff ear tags

The most important and frequently used numbers are listed below:

1st digit (thousands) – Position / nature

1 = standing

2 = lying

3 = sitting

4 = sitting up / begging / standing on back legs

5 = jointed

6 = young

7 = caricatured

8 = ball-jointed neck

9 = with clock-work mechanism

2nd digit (hundreds) – Type of material

1 = felt

2 = short-pile plush / coat plush

3 = mohair

4 = velvet

5 = lamb's wool plush / wool plush

6 = cellulose / artificial silk plush / dralon plush

7 = cotton fabric / oil cloth

8 = wood

9 = fur / metal

3rd & 4th digits (tens & ones) –

Size in cm, e.g.

10 = 10 cm

17 = 17 cm

35 = 35 cm etc.

Digit after the comma – Equipment / outfit

0 = without wheels

1 = soft filling / also: with squeaker

2 = automatic voice (growler) / double squeaker / cord-activated voice

3 = music-box

4 = simplified

5 = removable saddle

6 = tails / clothing

7 = muzzle / rucksack

8 = steering

9 = removable rocker

b = hot-water bottle (Wärmflasche)

ex = eccentric wheels (Exzenterräder)

H = neck mechanism / tail turns head (Halsmechanik)

ST = steering (Steuerung)

included in the Steiff product range. This very special bear has therefore always remained the sole property of Richard Steiff's family.

Already presented in seven sizes in 1905, "Bärle" is also offered in two new sizes with article numbers 5315 and 5325 in 1906. The number "1" added after the comma (soft filling) no longer appears for any of the nine available sizes in the catalogue. The weight of "Bärle" has remained the same and does not change until the growler is introduced in 1908. It must therefore be assumed that the soft filling, comprising a mixture of kapok and excelsior was still used up to 1907, at least, and that harder packed models were produced exclusively from 1908 onwards.

With the creation and presentation of "Bärle PAB" in 1905, the Teddy bear has been given an appearance that is to alter very little for many decades. Although different variations emerged over the years, the original Teddy has always remained in the product spectrum of Margarete Steiff GmbH.

Fig. 94: "Bärle" is available in nine different sizes.

The Steiff company and Design Patents

The design patent for the Bear 55PB is extended by three years on June 28th, 1906, i.e. up to 1909. Less than a year later, on February 20th, 1907, an application for another three-year extension is submitted to Heidenheim district court for the 35PB. These extensions may not appear to be particularly useful at first glance, particularly as neither bear is still included in the Steiff product range, but it seems likely that the applications were submitted purely as precautionary measures. At that time, the people at Steiff were still hoping to be able to obtain sole production rights for the jointed bear created within the company. This implies that the company not only intended to own the rights to produce current models, but also those for all previous versions of jointed bears. This assumption

Fig. 95: Front page of a design patent registration document dating back to 1903.

Fig. 96: Who could possibly resist such expressions?

would appear to be substantiated by the correspondence exchanged with patent lawyer Zeisig, who was instructed to register the patents, in 1908, i.e. before the terms of the patents for the two bears expired. Responding to a request for detailed information about the possibilities available to Margarete Steiff GmbH within the framework of design and utility-model patents and the costs involved, Mr. Zeisig wrote the following reply: "According to § 8 of the law relating to copyrights for designs and models dated January 11th, 1876, the originator of a design patent may be granted a period of protection amounting to between 1 and 3 years from the date of registration, as he wishes. When the three-year term of the patent has expired, the applicant may apply to extend the term of the patent up to 10 or 15 years from the day of registration. [...] This means that, assuming that you registered a design patent on August 7th, 1902, you could extend the term of the patent at the end of the initial three-year period by 3, 4, 5 years etc. as you wished, but the term cannot be extended again when the second period expires. [...] As, in your case, the third year has elapsed and the tenth cannot be reached, it is no longer possible to extend the design patent that you registered on August 7th, 1902, at this point in time. [...] The charges for protection of a design patent amount to 1 mark per year for every design or design package for the first three years. If the patent is extended up to 10 years, the charge increases to 2 marks per design between the third and tenth year and the annual charge for the 11th to 15th year amounts to 3 marks per design."

These statements are a clear indication that the Steiff company was already formulating concrete ideas regarding longer-term protection of designs. It was not until the term of the patent covering the felt dolls expired, which was the patent registered on August 7th, 1902, mentioned by the patent lawyer, that more precise information was obtained about the applicable terms and conditions.

It was not possible to extend the design patent protection for either the felt dolls or the jointed bear, however. There is little doubt that financial considerations also played a role initially, as the costs for longer-term design patents increased progressively with every additional year. It would certainly have been worthwhile as far as the felt dolls and, above all, our jointed Teddy bear, were concerned. The only alternative available was to draw attention to the fact that the Teddy bear was the sole creation of Steiff alone and to the first-class product quality that distinguished Steiff from the many rival firms that had appeared on the scene in the meantime.

Fig. 97

Fig. 98

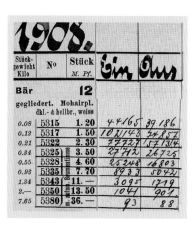

Fig. 99

THE STEIFF TEDDY BEAR'S MARCH OF CONQUEST

Fig. 97-99: Extracts from the production lists from 1906, 1907 and 1908.

The amazing number of 974,000 bears produced in 1907 is a well known, if inconceivable, figure mentioned in many publications.

The following table contains the actual figures for all of the bears sold between 1906 and 1908, broken down according to the different models. The relationship between the quantities of bears made in the various sizes has not changed a great deal, even in following years.

It is easy to see that the bears sold under article numbers 5317 and 5322 make up the lion's share of production as a whole with more than 70%. The absolute

A Brief Résumé of Teddy Bear's Creation

1901

Shiny plush, the mohair plush of today, is offered in the Steiff catalogue for the first time, exclusively for the 50 cm Bear on Wheels, which is available in brown, white and grey.

1902

Richard Steiff develops the first prototypes of the jointed bear made of shiny plush with Bear 55PB as its designation. One of these bears is shipped to America as a sales sample.

1903

Paul Steiff offers the bear to his American clients and the 55PB makes his first official appearance in Germany at the Leipzig Spring Trade Fair. The first illustration appears in the catalogue of new articles for 1903 and Bear 55PB is registered as a design copyright at Heidenheim district court on July 13th. There are no records of sales figures.

1904

The Bear 55PB is still the only bear offered in the Steiff catalogue dated February 1st.

Bear 35PB is registered as a design copyright at Heidenheim district court on March 5th. Steiff produces 12,000 bears throughout the year. The make-up of this figure is unknown, however. On December 6th, an application for a utility-model patent is registered for a "toy with movable limbs that are joined together with a twin wire which has closures inside the body of the toy".

1905

The design copyright for "Bärle 35PAB" ('P' for plush, 'A' for angescheibt (disk-jointed) and 'B' for beweglich (movable)) is registered on February 15th. His appearance corresponds to that of the well-known

58

Art.-Nr.	1906	1907	1908	1906-1908
5315	21.079	68.163	39.186	128.428
5317	182.102	398.928	74.857	655.887
5322	109.590	294.123	57.134	460.847
5325	24.113	106.524	26.725	157.362
5328	32.100	73.985	16.803	122.888
5335	10.864	22.224	5042	38.130
5343	3555	7249	1719	12.523
5350	1745	2482	901	5128
5380	245	321	88	664
	385.393	**973.999**	**222.455**	**1581.847**

Fig. 100: Steiff Teddy bears sold between 1905 and 1908 (summary).

favourite bears are those measuring 25 and 32 cm (measured standing). As far as the sales figures are concerned, larger and smaller bears just cannot keep up. This doesn't even change when tiny bears that are just 10 cm tall are added to the product range shortly afterwards. The same trend still applies today, 100 years later: the majority of bears on offer are between 25 and 35 cm tall.

Drawn up after 1908, the production lists are also broken down according to colour. They clearly indicate that the colour light brown, also referred to as blond, accounts for around 70% of the overall production figures, followed by white with up to 20% and dark brown lagging along behind with no more than 10%.

These figures are confirmed by the situation in the current collectors' market: most bears are made of blond mohair and are available in the sizes mentioned above. The "Bärle" reflects the final appearance that was to prove so important in the story of the Teddy bear's creation. Other models and variations that conquer the world over the following decades are presented in greater detail in the final section of this book.

Teddy bear of today. An application for a utility-model patent is registered for a "shaft or rod with projections forged out at the side to secure objects pushed onto it" is registered on June 8th. The bears offered in the Steiff catalogue dated August 15th includes the following models:

1. The new model, referred to as "Bärle PAB" available in seven sizes measured sitting down: 17, 22, 28, 35, 43, 50, 80 cm, and three different colours: light brown, dark brown and white. The article numbers for the new bears are 5317,1 to 5380,1.
2. The previous models of "Bärle", referred to as 28PB and 35PB (new article numbers 5328 and 5335). There are no details of the production figures for this year available.

1906

The Steiff collection no longer includes "Bärle PB". The Steiff product range now contains the new Teddy bear in two sizes with article numbers 5315 and 5325. 385,393 jointed bears are produced during the year.

1907

The record year for production of bears: Margarete Steiff GmbH sells nearly a million bears in total.

1908

Teddy bears of different sizes are added to the product spectrum. The bear is now also available with a growler.

Only 290,157 bears are produced this year, sales figures drop to 222,455 – a decline that can be attributed to the economic crisis in the USA. Teddy begins to establish himself in Europe as well, however, with the result that production can soon be resumed at full power. Even if the fantastic production figures from 1907 are still out of reach – there is now no way of stopping the worldwide success of the Teddy bear.

Fig. 101: Teddy bears dating back to between 1904 and 1910 – as we still know and love them today.

My Name is Teddy ...

AT LAST! THE JOINTED BEAR IS FINALLY GIVEN THE NAME THAT MILLIONS OF CHILDREN AND ADULTS ALL OVER THE WORLD ASSOCIATE WITH A CUDDLY ANIMAL THAT THEY LOVE AND ADMIRE TODAY.

Fig. 102: These two Teddy bears proudly present the coat of arms bearing the portrait of Theodore Roosevelt.

How did the Teddy bear actually come by his name? This is a question that is frequently asked and many of the familiar answers indicate a fairly vivid imagination on the part of everybody concerned.

This issue is a natural candidate for a great deal of speculation, of course, because unlike the history of the Teddy bear's development, there is no documentary evidence of the actual reason for this name being given to a bear.

The variety of answers and the ingenious ideas behind them have given rise to a number of wonderful stories. The version that follows is probably the most frequently related one as it has been used in a number of publications issued by Margarete Steiff GmbH for many years. It is certainly the most delightful story and, if it wasn't for the results of research conducted by the Steiff company and the Theodore Roosevelt Association in recent years, we could even have believed that it was true.

This story begins in November 1902, at around the time that Richard Steiff created the first jointed bear: the American President Theodore Roosevelt, a passion-

Fig. 103: On the trail of Theodore Roosevelt, Steiff Teddy bears hunting for bears ...

Fig. 104: Hunter or hunted? The Teddy family is also very resourceful in its natural habitat.

ately enthusiastic hunter, is invited to join a hunting party in the as yet unexplored Mississippi forests. The expedition goes on for several days and, in spite of the most vehement efforts on the part of the organisers, not a single bear is sighted. One of the scouts eventually finds and captures a very young bear (or was it weak with age?). The little Bruin is presented to the President for shooting, but Roosevelt refuses point blank to do so and even insists that the little bear is set free.

Clifford Berryman is another member of the VIP hunting party – a well-known American artist and caricaturist of his time. He captures the scene in a caricature which is published in the Washington Post a few days later.

This story increases the people's sympathy with the already very popular President tremendously. Clifford Berryman also becomes immensely popular, so it is hardly

Fig. 105: It goes against the President's honour to shoot a helpless bear. Caricature by Clifford Berryman – published in the Washington Post.

Fig. 106: Jointed elephants, donkeys and horses – but where on earth is my Teddy bear ...?

surprising that the well-liked shaggy little fellow is often to be found in his drawings in the period that follows. The little bear appears over and over again in the most diverse variations – and frequently in the company of Theodore Roosevelt. This unlikely pair becomes a real focal point of sympathetic interest, at least as far as the cartoons and associated humour and popular appeal are concerned.

The story is based on fact up to this point. It goes on to give an account of the forthcoming wedding of President Theodore Roosevelt's daughter in the White House in 1906. Something special is needed by way of decoration. As it happens, the company commissioned to organise the celebrations dispatches its representative to spend hours combing the streets of New York for something that has never been seen before.

Fig. 107

Theodore Roosevelt – the people's President

Theodore Roosevelt is born in New York City on October 27th, 1858, son of the wealthy businessman Theodore Roosevelt sen. and his wife Martha Roosevelt née Bulloch. During his childhood, he suffers from asthma so badly that he has to have private teachers for many of his lessons. He then attended Harvard College, where he graduated before moving on to Columbia Law School. He discontinues his law studies without taking a degree because,

after joining the Republican Party in 1880, he becomes the youngest member elected to the New York State Assembly in 1881. He makes a name for himself here with his strict attitude to corruption. A double tragedy hits Roosevelt in 1884 when his mother and his wife both die within hours of one another. Roosevelt withdraws from politics temporarily and publishes books instead.

Five years later in 1889, he heads the U.S. Civil Service Commission before resigning in 1895 and is finally appointed as

Fig. 108: Teddy bears as table decorations
– a lovely story – but unfortunately ...

The envoy's luck finally changes when he reaches FAO Schwarz, the toy shop. Catching sight of the Steiff bears on show there, he is immediately reminded of the Berryman caricatures. Just what he has been looking for!

Dressed up in hunting and fishing gear, the bears are arranged on the tables along with miniature tents, campfires and other suitable accessories. The decorations are a complete success: the wedding party is more than enthusiastic at the sight of the enchanting Steiff bears.

President of the Board of Police Commissioners, New York City in the same year. Two years later, he is appointed Assistant Secretary of the Navy by William McKinley, the President of the USA. Popular as a result of his exploits during the Spanish-American War, he is elected as Governor of New York State. In this capacity, he instigates comprehensive political reforms. Elected as Vice President in 1900, he takes over the office of President when William McKinley is murdered in 1901. As far as home affairs are concerned, his presidency is marked by successful mediation between the various business interests and restrictions on privately motivated destructive exploitation of resources, preserving natural resources in particular (an early environmentalist!). In terms of foreign policy, Roosevelt's most impressive achievements are to terminate America's isolation from Europe and his ambition to make the USA the leading power for the American continent as a whole. He is awarded the Nobel Peace Prize for ending the Russo-Japanese War in 1905. In spite of his tremendous popularity among the American people, he does not stand as a candidate for a third term of office in the 1909 election, devoting his attention to private affairs for a while before returning to politics. During the 1st World War he is among the advocates of America's entry into the war and he speaks out vehemently in favour of a foreign policy that is oriented to the Allies. Theodore Roosevelt dies at his home in Oyster Bay/New York on January 6th, 1919.

Fig. 109: Theodore Roosevelt is also honoured in Teddy bear's home town – bronze bust in the Steiff Museum.

At some stage during the evening – the guests have already started relating tall stories about their hunting escapades – someone puts a question to the President: "Mr. President, you're an outstanding huntsman and you're a real authority on bears – what breed do you think the bears on the table belong to?" Theodore Roosevelt hesitates for a moment before answering and another of the guests steps in, his tongue probably loosened slightly by champagne: "Well, that's obvious, they're Teddy bears." (This deduction alludes to the customary abbreviation of the President's name – Theodore is shortened to Teddy.) All of the guests roared with laughter at this fitting statement and the name Teddy bear was born.

The second part of the story above can only be regarded as a legend. After all, the research conducted by both the Theodore Roosevelt Association and Margarete Steiff GmbH has determined without any shadow of doubt that, at the time in question, there was no wedding and no table decorations with Teddy bears in the White House. A fairytale, too wonderful to be true ...

ROOSEVELT AND THE TEDDY BEAR: THE BEGINNING OF AN ETERNAL FRIENDSHIP

If that is not the way it happened, what else could have turned the bear into a Teddy bear? Theodore Roosevelt undoubtedly holds the key to the mystery. Published over and over again, Clifford Berryman's caricatures showing the President in the company of the little bear, who has also become quite famous in the meantime, lead to the development of a relationship of sorts between two of the popular figures in this era.

The people of America are enthralled, and having one of these cute, cuddly bears has now almost become a mark of good breeding, particularly as Teddy is such good friends with the President. Our Teddy bear therefore not only captures the hearts of the children for whom he is originally intended soon after putting in his first appearance, but also finds a place in the hearts of many adults. And this is still true today.

Roosevelt's descendants still maintain close contact with Margarete Steiff GmbH. A big party was held in Giengen, the Teddy bear's birthplace, in 1958 to celebrate the former American President's 100th birthday. And on occasions like this, such as the 90th birthday of the Teddy bear in 1992, the current representatives of this family that has such importance in world history are always welcome guests of honour.

Fig. 110: Tweed Roosevelt, one of Theodore Roosevelt's great-grandsons unveils the bronze statue to commemorate the 90th birthday of the Teddy bear created by Richard Steiff.

Fig. 111: Teddy Roosevelt together with the new President, Billy Possum (William Taft).

Members of the Roosevelt family are also drawn to Giengen to attend the Steiff Festival that has been held once a year since 1997.

The bronze bust of Theodore Roosevelt that was unveiled on his 100th birthday is on show in the Steiff Museum.

As the Roosevelt family chronicles still relate today, the abundance of sketches that Clifford Berryman made of President Theodore Roosevelt led to a relationship approaching friendship that developed between the two men. Although the President was not particularly enthusiastic about the caricature with the bear initially – being published in conjunction with articles reporting on the failure of the

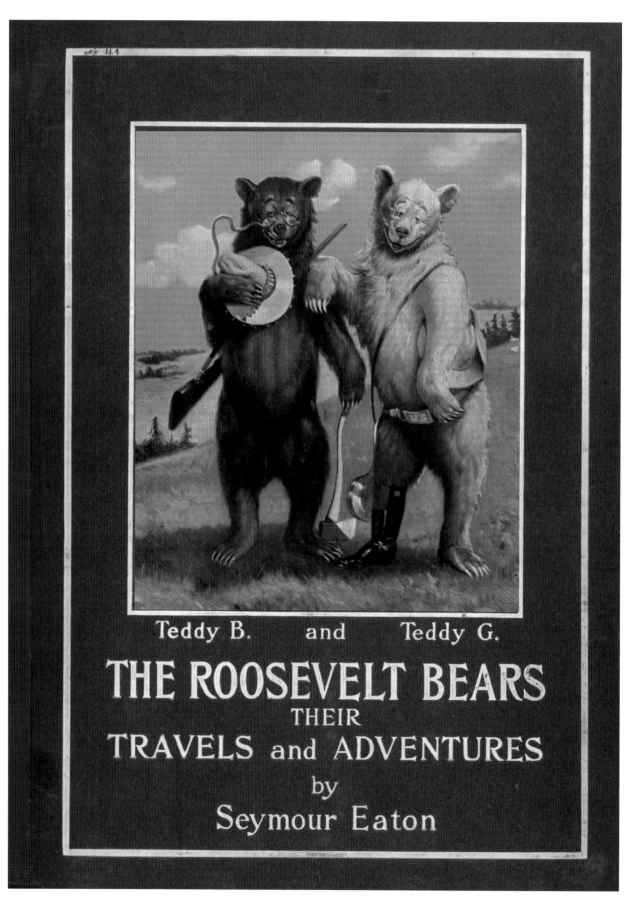

Fig. 112: Front cover of the book by Seymour Eaton.

hunting trip as a whole, Roosevelt soon discovers that it generates a liking for him among the people of his country. Being an intelligent statesman and politician, he appreciates this popularity: whenever Roosevelt is jovially and affectionately confronted with Teddy bears on the most diverse occasions throughout his period of office – he is quite happy to play along.

When Roosevelt passes the presidency on to William Howard Taft, the 27th President of the United States of America, in 1909, Steiff celebrates the occasion by building a wonderful scene with Steiff dolls and animals and captures it on film. The retiring President Roosevelt, represented by a Teddy bear of course, welcomes his successor, William H. Taft, nicknamed Billy Possum and played by a possum (refer to Fig. 111 on page 69).

Duplicity of events: Steiff's possum came nowhere near to achieving the same success as the Teddy bear – and President Taft never managed to achieve the same political or personal success as his predecessor Theodore Roosevelt ...

Fig. 113: Steiff's possum cannot match the success of the Teddy bear.

TEDDY B AND TEDDY G:
THE ADVENTURE OF THE ROOSEVELT BEARS

The Roosevelt family chronicles make no mention of the exact time at which the familiar form of the Presidents first name "Teddy" was combined with the animal name "bear" to produce the "Teddy bear". The name of the person who created this neologism also remains a mystery. One thing is certain, however, and that is that the term was coined in America and it was used for the first time somewhere between 1905 and 1907.

This is also implied by the following publication, for example: in September 1906, Edward Stern & Company Inc. of Philadelphia publishes the stories of Teddy B and Teddy G in a book entitled "The Roosevelt Bears – their travels and adventures" by Seymour Eaton with illustrations by V. Floyd Campbell.

Fig. 114 right: Steiff also produced a Teddy G as early as 1907.

Fig. 115: Stereotype drawing of Baho on all four legs.

Used here, the B in Teddy B does not stand for Bear, however, but for one of the following English words: "black or brown, bright or bold or brave or boss". Eaton explains the G in Teddy G as standing for "grizzly or grey or gay". Completely in line with the style of these entertaining and affectionately composed stories, Teddy B explicitly draws the reader's attention to the fact that B does not stand for bad and G does not stand for good.

The copyright registered for Seymour Eaton dates back to 1905 because, as he states in his foreword, stories about Teddy B and

Teddy G had already been published as serials in 20 daily newspapers. Incidentally, the records show that President Roosevelt was quite happy about the way in which his name was used.

Although the Teddy bear name never actually appears in that form in Seymour Eaton's stories, the name to be adopted in the near future is indicated by the fact that the word "Teddy" is used in the names of the two protagonists, and in connection with the "Roosevelt Bears" mentioned in the title of the book.

Even if we still don't know the date on which the Teddy bear designation was used for the first time or the name of the person who thought the name up – these facts and figures are of little importance to the actual Teddy bear and his worldwide success.

Fig. 116: Bear
with muzzle.

STEIFF'S TEDDY BEAR

The first mention of our protagonist's name within the Steiff company is particularly interesting as the term "Teddy bear" was not used there until much later. In February 1908, for example, the translated wording of a leaflet issued for the Spring Trade Fair is as follows: "We are sending you a price list covering our Steiff soft animals in good time for the trade fair. It includes the original series of Teddy bears with growlers at new reduced prices. [...] We are the sole originators of the jointed bears that have become world famous under the name 'Teddy bears', which means that neither the model nor the idea comes from America."

Fig. 117: The catalogue photograph of Teddy bear 5380 was used between 1906 and 1908.

Fig. 118: Trade fair publication from 1908. Margarete Steiff refuses to let anyone else take the credit for inventing the Teddy bear.

Fig. 119: Cuddly pleasure!

Wouldn't everyone like to join in?

These words clearly indicate that Steiff's competitors wanted to have a share in the Teddy bear's success by that time. The lead over rival companies is accentuated by the emphasis on the "Original Teddy bear" wording and the unequivocal reference to Steiff being the sole inventor. If the toy company was unable to obtain the industrial property rights for the Teddy bear name, the world should at least be told which Teddy bear is the genuine article. This offered a means of ruining business for unwanted rivals.

Nobody argued either; neither in response to the unambiguous declaration of Steiff's claim to sole authorship on the Teddy bear, nor to the publication in the USA described below.

Although Margarete Steiff GmbH never shied away from asserting the company's rights in a court of law if necessary (as documented in many other instances), there are no records that indicate that the declaration of authorship was ever discussed or even contested in the Steiff archive or in the complete records of Heidenheim district court, which was the place of jurisdiction for legal matters of this nature. The earliest known American publication in which Steiff uses the name Teddy bear dates back to August 1908, when the following article containing a letter from Margarete Steiff appeared in the Children's Magazine in America under the heading "About the inventor of the Teddy bear". Referring to this letter, she said: "Many thousands of American children love Teddy bears, so they will enjoy reading this letter from Germany, written by the industrious lady who invented and produced the very first Teddy."

To the children in America:

Dear children, would you like to find out how the Teddy bear came into being? Listen to me and I'll tell you all about it.

I was already in the habit of making toys for my many nephews and nieces thirty years ago. All of these toys were modelled on various animals. The children really put them to the test, taking the toys, throwing them up into the air and letting them drop to the ground before picking them up again. Almost breathless with exertion, the children used to come back to me and tell me how amazed they were that toys had not broken in spite of the heavy fall.

This made me decide to devote all of my attention to making toys that children could neither break nor destroy and this idea was received with great applause all round. I was soon unable to satisfy the demands of all of the little boys and girls who were waiting for one of my toy animals on my own. I had to employ people to help me and my menagerie gradually became larger and more complete.

When my nephews were grown up, we built a large factory where many industrious hands now work to produce all types of toy animals. Four years ago, I managed to make the jointed bear into the most popular children's toy. This bear was then given the name "Teddy bear" for the first time in America.

I recently had postcards printed that show a delightful family of bears. I will send one of these pictures to every child who sends me his or her address and I would be particularly delighted to receive lots of letters from American children.

Affectionate greetings to all of you from the Teddy bear's auntie

Margarete Steiff
from Giengen an der Brenz in Germany

Fig. 120: The photograph on the left is published in the Children's Magazine in 1908, accompanied by a letter written by Margarete Steiff.

Fig. 121: One of the most delightful photographs ever taken: time for the bear dance.

Fig. 122: Cards like this are much sought-after by collectors and fetch top prices at auction. This one has Margarete Steiff's original signature on the reverse side and fetched more than US$ 2,270 at the auction held during the 4th Steiff Festival in 2000.

Many of the wonderful postcards showing the most diverse scenes composed of Steiff animals and dolls also go back to this period. The postcard showing a family of bears that Margarete Steiff promised the American children as a reward for writing to her was also one of these.

Margarete Steiff's letter would be described as direct marketing nowadays. An action that was necessary for the following reason: Teddy bear business had declined drastically as a consequence of the 1908 economic crisis in America, which meant that efforts had to be made to promote the company's products. Paul Steiff's notes on this subject contain the following reference: "It was Richard Steiff's wish, aim, endeavour, success to establish correspondence, acquaintance, knowledge, trade etc. with Americ. customers, consumers & children with M.St. toys & listen to what they say about his bear that became known as the Teddy bear

Fig. 123:
This scene showing bears from the Baho
series is extremely life-like.

Fig. 124:

Grumpy or forceful – Baho always cuts
a good figure.

after May 1903! Because his Aunt Marg. did not believe in animals made of
expensive mohair plush as they are more highly priced than her animals that have
been made of felt since 1880."

Paul Steiff's mention of the year 1903 is particularly interesting. He must have made
his notes from memory as the article "About the inventor of the Teddy bear" did not
appear in the Children's Magazine until August 1908. It seems hardly likely that he
could have mistaken the date by two years, but apart from this handwritten note by
Paul Steiff, there are no other records to indicate that the name "Teddy bear" was
used so early. Oh well, perhaps the Teddy bear will reveal this part of his history during the second century of his existence, which is just starting ...

The Teddy bear name is first used in an official Steiff catalogue in 1913, when it
appears in the catalogue of new articles for that year. The "Record-Teddy auf

Fig. 125 left: A beautiful arrangement of clothed Teddy bears, this
photograph was taken in Steiff's
own studio.

Fig. 126: This stereotype drawing
shows Basa preparing for his appearance in the 1908 catalogue.

Selbstfahrer" (a Teddy on a unit that moves automatically when pulled) is listed under the heading Teddy Bear. Although the main 1913 catalogue again refers to bears in general – after all, the product spectrum still includes bears without moving limbs, such as the bears on wheels, riding bears and dancing bears – all of the Steiff catalogues issued afterwards use the name Teddy bear to refer to all of the various versions of jointed bears.

The 1920s finally saw the use of such advertising slogans as "Teddy bear – The world-famous Steiff invention, every child's favourite toy", "First name in soft-filled toys – Inventor of the Teddy bear" or "Teddy – this Steiff invention has lost none of its great popularity up to now" to promote sales of the jointed bear. And as far as we are concerned, in the present day and age, it is virtually impossible to imagine that there was ever a time when our Teddy wasn't called Teddy.

Fig. 127: Aftro is the name of the mohair plush monkey wearing a sweater, trousers and hat.

Fig. 128: These clothed monkeys are further examples of product diversity.

Fig. 129: There's certainly something going on in the Steiff Zoo – all "Original Steiff Products", both inside and outside the cages.

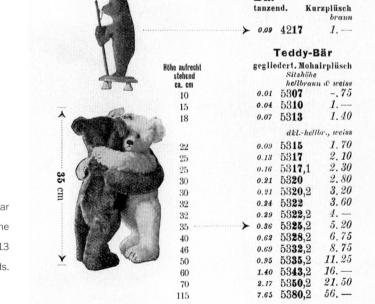

Fig. 130: The name Teddy bear is used for jointed bears in the Steiff catalogue from 1913 onwards.

Bär

tanzend. Kurzplüsch
braun

0.09	4217	1.—

Teddy-Bär

gegliedert. Mohairplüsch

Höhe aufrecht stehend ca. cm			*Sitzhöhe hellbraun & weiss*
10	0.01	5307	-.75
15	0.04	5310	1.—
18	0.07	5313	1.40
			dkl.-hellbr., weiss
22	0.09	5315	1.70
25	0.13	5317	2.10
25	0.16	5317,1	2.30
30	0.21	5320	2.80
30	0.21	5320,2	3.20
32	0.24	5322	3.60
32	0.29	5322,2	4.—
35	0.36	5325,2	5.20
40	0.62	5328,2	6.75
46	0.69	5332,2	8.75
50	0.95	5335,2	11.25
60	1.40	5343,2	16.—
70	2.17	5350,2	21.50
115	7.65	5380,2	56.—

From Model to Series Production

VI.

MORE THAN 100 YEARS OF EXPERIENCE AND MANY INDUSTRIOUS AND PROFICIENT PAIRS OF HANDS ARE INVOLVED IN PUTTING THE LARGE NUMBER OF INDIVIDUAL PIECES TOGETHER IN NUMEROUS OPERATIONS TO CREATE A STEIFF TEDDY BEAR FOR SERIES PRODUCTION.

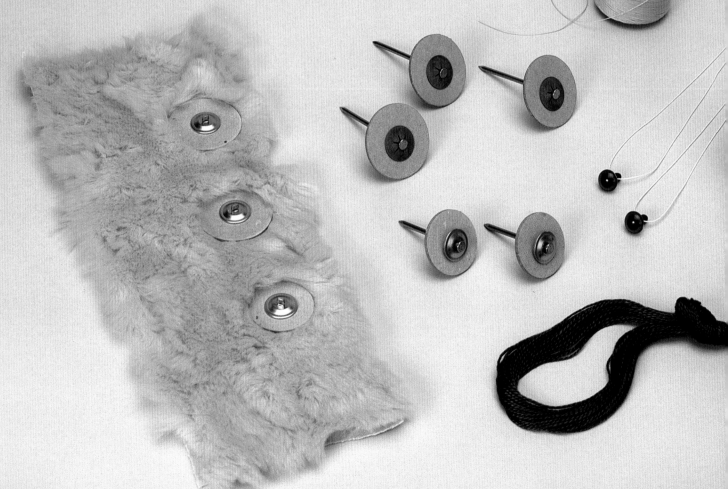

Figs. 131 and 132:
Materials used in the production of plush animals at Steiff
and the finished product:
the Teddy bear.

A tremendous amount of interest is always shown whenever there is an opportunity to get an insight into the manufacturing process of Steiff animals. Long queues always build up in front of the various workplaces in the manufacturing demonstration at the annual Steiff Festival in Giengen, for example, or during the Steiff Convention in Baden-Baden.

Irrespective of the stage in the process – cutting out, sewing, stuffing with excelsior or finishing – the experienced members of staff from Margarete Steiff GmbH patiently answer the many questions that reflect some of the more unusual and eccentric ideas and imaginations of the bear enthusiasts. Countless visitors are always astounded by the fact that most of the operations involved in producing a Steiff animal are still performed by hand, even today.

It goes without saying that modern technology is also used at Steiff wherever possible nowadays. There are no offices without computers, no handling without appropriate high-tech equipment, no packaging facility without the use of state-of-the-art technology – and the designers use the most up-to-date software to assist them in the development of new toy animals. Skilful, well-trained hands are what are needed in the manufacturing process, however, and have been for more than 100 years, because they offer the only means of meeting the stringent requirements of the self-imposed, high quality standard. After all, a manufactory – which is what Margarete Steiff GmbH is – relies on manual production stages and the same result cannot be achieved with an assembly line.

To the same extent as 100 years of Teddy bears have not been made of any old materials; they need soft, glossy, hard-wearing coats in order to develop their very own inherent charisma.

Fig. 133: Insight into the fabric store at Margarete Steiff GmbH. Apparently endless aisles filled with the stuff that dreams are made of, packed close together and piled up high.

Fig. 134: The staff of Margarete Steiff GmbH demonstrating the individual stages required to produce a Steiff animal according to the old tradition before the eyes of a fascinated audience.

Fig. 135: The Steiff archive is not only the home of Steiff animals. It also accommodates patterns, templates, tools and the complete know-how gathered over more than 100 years of company history.

The shelves in the material store on the premises of Margarete Steiff GmbH are therefore still piled high with rolls of mohair plush in the most diverse shades and finishes. The multifarious mohair plush fabrics kept here include those with long and short pile, some with greater density than others, tipped, smooth and curly. In other words: whatever one's heart desires – the choice is enormous.

The following description of the various stages in a Teddy bear's production is intended to give an insight into the working techniques still practised within the Steiff company today.

Development of a model bear

The shape, materials and details must have already been specified before the parts of the bear can be cut out. This is the work performed by the developers, pattern designers and the staff in the operations scheduling department. They use their creative ideas and draw on many years of experience to develop the individual components of the Teddy, piece by piece, to produce the complete bear – fashioned completely in accordance with the concept of Richard Steiff, who set an example 100 years ago.

Everything must fit together. The proportions must be correct to the same extent as the general impression given by the bear; the colours of plush and stitching must harmonise with one another and the eyes must not clash with the materials used or the shades used for decorative stitching or finishing ... these are just a few of the details to be taken into consideration. The process leading up to a model bear is marked by a whole series of different variations and a sample of each version is produced exclusively by hand.

When the designer – the name used to describe the developer today – is finally satisfied with the result, he presents his design to a committee which is responsible for its final acceptance and adoption. Made up of members of staff from the various departments, including production, marketing, purchasing and sales, this committee joins forces with the development department to decide whether the newly developed bear is to be added to the Steiff product range and, if so, whether any changes need to be made.

If a decision is made in favour of the newly designed bear, he is given a genuine Steiff "Button in Ear" and a very special ear tag. This tag bears the inscription "HANDMUSTER", which is German for "hand sample", and confirms that the bear with the tag is the very first approved model of a new series.

All other designs and models produced prior to this are then destroyed to ensure that only the hand sample remains from this point onwards. Ten other samples are subsequently made, which are exact copies of the hand sample. These are destined for

Fig. 136 left: Steiff tags for approved designer models.

Fig. 137 right: Steiff tags for type samples in the production department.

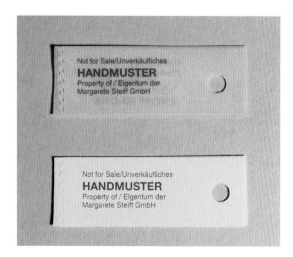

Fig. 138: Paul Steiff's workshop cabinet. The tools that it holds are no longer state-of-the-art, of course. But the story that this piece of furniture reveals and the inscriptions branded in the wood by Paul Steiff himself give the observer a sense of the atmosphere of days gone by.

the various departments which use them as models throughout the different stages of production. These bears are also given Steiff buttons and special tags – this time bearing the German word "WERKMUSTER", which means "type sample".

Exact material plans – referred to as parts lists – and precise manufacturing schedules are drawn up at the same time; after all, every detail counts. The manufacturing schedule specifies that all parts must be cut out with the correct pile direction, for example, to ensure that Teddy's hair doesn't "stand on end". It goes without saying that attention is also given to preventing the precious materials being wasted unnecessarily when cutting out.

85

Fig. 139: The screen with the pattern for the Teddy bear is filled out with paint ...

The next stage involves ordering materials from the relevant suppliers. Such necessary auxiliaries as templates, punching dies etc. are made on the premises or ordered, as applicable. Production cannot commence until all of the source materials and tools are available.

The template, an indispensable tool, is required to prepare the mohair plush for cutting out. In the course of manufacturing, the Teddy bear pattern is transferred to a large metal plate with a row of tiny holes punched along the contours of each individual piece. An initial coat of paint is applied to the resulting screen with a soft squeegee to prevent it smearing in the subsequent stages and it is then placed on the reverse side of the plush, which is secured to long tables with tensioning devices. New paint is then applied continuously, mapping the pattern pieces onto the mohair, piece by piece.

Fig. 140: ... the pattern is transferred onto the reverse side of the mohair.

Fig. 141: The individual components are cut out along the lines printed onto the pieces of mohair.

Fig. 142: The pile must not be damaged during the cutting process.

Fig. 143 top: The woollen felt is spread out on the punching machine.

Fig. 144 right: A punching die is used to cut out the pieces that are needed.

CUTTING OUT

The individual pieces are cut out of the plush, using scissors to cut along the contour lines. Only the backing fabric should be cut as the bear would have noticeable bald patches along the seams if the pile were to be damaged. The paw linings and the soles of Teddy's feet are made of fine woollen felt. This material does not have a long pile, which means that the felt pieces can be simply punched out without having to exercise the care required when cutting plush. A metal punching die of the right shape is made and clamped into the punching machine that works at very high pressure. This method of cutting out enables a great deal of time to be saved at this stage of the production process.

Fig. 145: Dexterity is the key when
sewing the various pieces together.

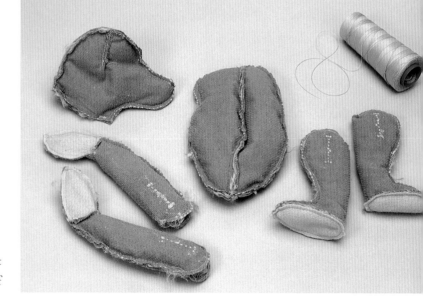

IN THE SEWING ROOM ...

... all of the cut-out and stamped pieces are brought
together for further processing. A total of 23 pieces of
felt and mohair are sewn together here like a jigsaw
puzzle to produce Teddy's outer skin. This then consists of six separate sections:
the body, the arms and legs and the head. All of the pieces are sewn together inside
out to ensure that the seams are not immediately visible from the outside. With a
little imagination, it is already possible to see a Teddy bear emerging from the sections that have been sewn together here.

Extremely dextrous, nimble fingers (ten at least) are needed to ensure that the pile
is always stroked into the seam while sewing and still manoeuvre round the tigh-
test curve. The speed and confidence with which the seamstresses work is really
quite amazing.

Fig. 146: This is what Teddy looks like when
the seamstress has finished her work.

Fig. 147: This is where the individual sections of the Teddy bear are turned the right way round with the mohair on the outside.

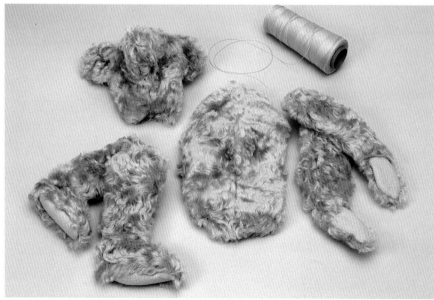

Fig. 148: Our Teddy bear may be furry, but he still looks rather thin when the pieces have been turned the right way round.

When the individual pieces have been sewn together the sections are turned the right way round so that the "pretty" side of the mohair is visible. This task becomes increasingly difficult, however, as the pieces get smaller. Our Teddy bear still looks fairly thin at the end of this stage, but that will soon change ...

Fig. 149: The Teddy bear is given his final shape when stuffed with excelsior.

Fig. 150: The next stage involves joining the finished parts together.

BREATHING LIFE INTO TEDDY

Most of the work leading up to this stage in the production process is performed by women, as there are few men whose naturally larger and stronger hands have sufficient dexterity and skill for such intricate tasks. Things are very different in the stuffing room. Muscle power is what is required here, as well as sensitivity. Men are usually responsible for giving the Teddy bear his plump excelsior stuffing. They make sure that the excelsior is firmly and evenly packed into the most inaccessible, tiniest areas so that Teddy doesn't have to go through life with any unattractive dents or humps.

Muscle power alone is not enough, however, the excelsior packer must also have the necessary experience at his disposal; after all, it is his work that adds shape to the final appearance of the bear. One tool that has proven to be extremely useful in this work is a piece of wood that looks rather like a small, flattened baseball bat. It is used to knock the Teddy into the right shape from time to time.

If the packer doesn't have the necessary instinctive feel and pushes the stuffing tool through the mohair plush, then there is no way of repairing the damage.

It's therefore no wonder that the Teddy bear starts growling in the hands of the packer ... Having half-filled the body of the bear, the packer fits the growler and buries it in the rest of the stuffing that fills the remaining body cavity. After all,

Fig. 151 top: The eyes are finally drawn into the Teddy bear's head.

Fig. 152 right: The hand-stitched nose, mouth and claws gives the Teddy his personality.

Fig. 153: Quality certificate awarded to Margarete Steiff GmbH by the Bavarian District Court Factory Inspectorate.

it must not be possible to feel or even see any edges or corners when the bear is finished.

Firm cardboard and metal disks are then fitted into the filled body, arms, legs and head. The seams that have been left open for this are then sewn up. These hand-stitched seams are always in the same place on each section.

The limbs and head are subsequently attached to the body with split pins that join two mating disks together. These Teddybear joints bring movement onto the scene – thanks to a technique that was first applied nearly 100 years ago in the PAB bear series.

FINAL TOUCHES: THE SERIES-PRODUCED TEDDY ON THE TEST BENCH

Almost completed, the Teddy bear is now "garnished" in a process that we normally associate with the catering industry. And this term really is appropriate: like the decorative elements that a good chef adds to finish off a creatively prepared meal, Teddy is given the important little final touches that will characterise his final appearance. His nose, mouth and claws are stitched by hand – as evenly as possible. The glass eyes are then fitted and their positions play a crucial role. The threads securing the eyes are led through the head and they are then

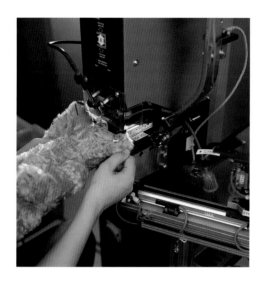

Fig. 154: Special tongs were originally used to attach the Steiff button in Teddy's ear. This job is now performed by a machine that was specially developed for this purpose.

pulled tight and knotted together at the back of the head. If a Teddy's eyes are too close together, they give him a grim expression and he appears apathetic if they are too far apart. The bear even squints if they are fitted asymmetrically. And who wants a squinting bear?

The final station in a Teddy's production is the beauty parlour. Each seam is examined again because the pile of the mohair plush occasionally gets trapped during the sewing operation. If this is the case, the hairs are carefully pulled out of the seam and brushed in the right direction. Any loose fibres and remnants of fabric are removed from his coat, which is then brushed up to free it of any remaining bits of fluff. And there he is!

Teddy still has one final hurdle to take, however, and that is the test bench. The safety, harmlessness to health, suitability for use and quality of every article in the Steiff toy collection is tested and monitored continuously by the Bavarian District Court Factory Inspectorate (abbreviated to LGA in German) within the framework of a surveillance agreement. The LGA quality certificate is issued to prove this. Any item that also stands up to the critical eyes of the quality controllers at Margarete Steiff GmbH and is found to be absolutely faultless is rewarded with something that distinguishes him and all of his ancestors from every other Teddy bear and has been doing since November 1st, 1904: the famous little button (with the accompanying tag) is attached to his ear, marking him as an "Original Steiff Teddy".

He can then set off on his journey into the world outside, bringing pleasure to young and old alike. Whether toy or collector's item, the Teddy bear faithfully performs the duties assigned to him.

Fig. 155: Isn't he wonderful? Unmistakably a Steiff Teddy bear – produced by hand with loving attention to detail.

92

What the Teddy Bear Means to Young and Old

WHY ON EARTH HAS OUR MOST FAITHFUL
PLAYTIME COMPANION BEEN MODELLED
ON SUCH A DREADED WILD BEAST OF PREY?

LOOKING BACK ON THE STORY
OF INDOMITABLE BEARS AND
THEIR POINTS OF CONTACT
WITH THE HUMAN RACE.

Fig. 156: The bear – a dreaded
beast of prey.

Fig. 157: The Teddy bear –
our most faithful playmate ...

Fig. 158: Teddy bears are simply adorable – hard to believe when you look at their wild relatives in the animal kingdom.

Although man and bear have been living together on the earth for thousands of years, no friendships have ever been established between the largest living land predator and human beings. For a long time, Mister Bruin was even regarded as being one of man's most dreaded enemies and terrible fights to the death were not unusual in the struggle to acquire or defend food or habitat.

Later attempts to subjugate or even domesticate bears also proved unsuccessful. Even "tame" circus bears never cease to be dangerous beasts of prey, in spite of being brought up in captivity after being left by their mothers as cubs. Their behaviour can change in a fraction of a second, transforming the putative clumsy giant into a nimble and powerful aggressor.

So how on earth did the brown bear, this dreaded wild predator, become the model for our most devoted playtime companion, the Teddy bear?

In spite of all of the natural differences distinguishing man from beast, there are certain common factors. Anybody studying young bear cubs will notice certain similarities because, like young children, they put everything they can get their hands (or paws) on in their mouths and they do this with their front paws in the same way as a human child. Furthermore, brown bears are also capable of walking on their hind legs – a skill not shared by many other animal species. Walking upright is not only a demonstration of strength and pride for human beings: the bear won't be tamed by anyone, it is not in his nature to play a subservient role.

The bear's strength and self-confidence have obviously always impressed mankind. According to Siberian tradition, there have been ceremonies, hunting rites and even celebrations in honour of the bear. Over 1000 years ago, some people firmly believed that the bear's hide accommodated a human being with divine power and wisdom.

According to the Germanic religion, even saying the word "bear" was forbidden as it was regarded as being sacred. The Celts worshipped the bear as a symbol of fertility.

Fig. 159: Even Homer referred to the constellation of the Great Bear in his Odyssey.

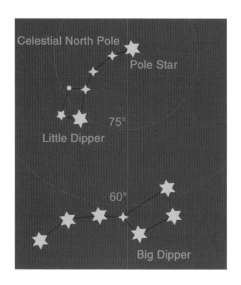

Fig. 160: The Plough or Big and Little Dippers.

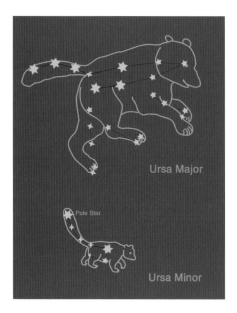

Fig. 161: Ursa Major and Ursa Minor (including the surrounding stars).

GREAT BEAR AND LITTLE BEAR – THE STARS IN THE HEAVENS

Greek mythology and the legends of certain tribes of North American Indians deliver fascinating accounts of how constellations came into being in connection with bears.

Everybody must be familiar with the Great Bear and Little Bear – with their Latin names Ursa Major and Ursa Minor – shining up in the night sky. They were originally known as just the Great Bear or Plough. A reference is even made to the names Bear and wain (an earlier word for plough) in the 5th book of Homer's Odyssey, which was written around 800 years before Christ. The following lines are taken from the translation by Samuel Butler:

> *"... while he sat and guided the raft skilfully by means of the rudder. He never closed his eyes, but kept them fixed on the Pleiades, on late-setting Bootes and on the Bear – which men also call the wain, and which turns round and round where it is, facing Orion, and alone never dipping into the stream of Oceanus – for Calypso had told him to keep this to his left."*

Measuring 1280 square degrees, the Great Bear is the third largest constellation in the skies and the Plough that it contains is the best generally known. When winter comes to an end and turns into spring and the constellation is high in the sky, the whole bear with his head and front and rear paws stands out very well on a clear dark night.

The seven brightest stars of the Great Bear make up the so-called Plough or Big Dipper. Aratos of Soloi (310 to 245 BC) was the first astronomer to add the surrounding stars to produce the image of a bear walking on its hind legs with its front paws on top of one another.

The Odyssey makes no mention of the Little Bear, the classical constellation that is also referred to as the Little Dipper. This was purportedly first measured 600 years before Christ by Thales of Miletus who is frequently credited with various theorems of elementary geometry. According to Aratos, the Achaeans sailed towards the Great Bear, whereas the Phoenicians sailed towards the Little Bear because it is closer to the celestial pole.

Fig. 162: Steiff was already producing Red Indian felt dolls in 1911.

BEARY STORIES

According to one legend, Zeus, the king and father of the gods, fell in love with Callisto, daughter of the cruel King Lycaon of Arcadia. Callisto bore him a son named Arcas. When Hera, the violently jealous wife of Zeus, found out about her husband's love affair, she turned Callisto into a bear. One day, Arcas, who had grown up into a skilful huntsman in the meantime, met his mother who was in the form of the bear. She recognised her son, but could only growl at him in greeting and raised herself on her hind legs to embrace him with joy. But Arcas only saw a she-bear rearing menacingly on her hind legs and threatening him with her sharp claws and teeth ... Zeus just arrived in time to stop Arcas killing his mother. He then transformed Arcas into another bear, grasped both bears by their tails and hurled them up into the heavens – Callisto became the Great Bear and Arcas the Little Bear. This story also explains why the two heavenly bears have such long tails, unlike their mortal relatives.

The Kiowa, a tribe of North American Indians, relate another story about a bear: seven sisters were playing with their only brother in the forest. The little boy suddenly began to tremble and crawling about on all fours. Hair started sprouting all over his body and his fingers and toes turned into claws. He was finally completely transformed into a bear. His sisters were frightened and ran away from him. The bear chased after them. They came to a tree that called to the little girls and told them to climb its trunk. While they were doing this, the tree began to grow. The bear could no longer reach the sisters and angrily tore the bark of the tree to shreds. But the tree carried the seven little girls up to heaven, where they took their places as the stars in the Plough or Big Dipper.

Other Indian nations, such as the Iroquois, referred to Ursa Major and Ursa Minor as "Okuri" and "Paukunawa", which both mean bear. According to their mythology, all bears used to have long tails. One day, however, the earthly bear was trying to catch fish through a hole in the ice covering a frozen lake. The hole froze over as well, though, with the bear's tail stuck fast. The bear then ripped his own tail off in his attempts to free himself. Mortal bears have only had short, stumpy tails ever since.

Fig. 163: The mythology of the North American Indians also tells many stories about the creation of constellations that include references to bears.

THE BEAR AS A SYMBOL
OF AUTHORITY AND STRENGTH

The Greek word for bear is "arktos" – and the term "arctic" was actually derived
from it. Both constellations – Great Bear and Little Bear – are always visible from
the Arctic Circle. The seven stars that make up the Plough or Big Dipper and the
Pole Star were therefore chosen as the motif for the national flag of Alaska, the
northernmost state in the USA.

A bear is also the symbol for the capital city of Germany – and has been for a long
time. The earliest verifiable use of the bear in connection with Berlin dates back to
the year 1280, when it appeared on a seal for the City of Berlin – which was not
officially founded until 1237 – stamped onto the document establishing the Berlin

Figs. 164-166: Steiff's Berlin Bears ...

top left: ... from 1993.

bottom left: 1997 Berliner Schutz-
mann Bear [Berlin constable].

right: ... from 1985.

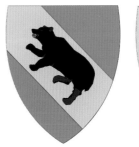

Fig. 167: Alaska's national flag with
the seven stars of the Plough or Big
Dipper and the Pole Star.

Fig. 168: Berlin's current coat of arms.

Figs. 169 and 170: Bears also appear
on the coats of arms of Swiss cities
Bern and St. Gallen.

Fig. 171: Bears play the leading roles in
many fairytales written by the Brothers
Grimm.

furriers' guild. This means that the bear was already adorning the Berlin coats of arms more than 700 years ago. Apparent evidence for the deep respect and esteem shown to the bear at that time. Its image served to demonstrate the authority, prestige and power of whoever used it.

There are allegedly 200 towns with names that can be traced back to the bear (Bär) in Germany alone: Bärstadt, Bärenklau and Bärenwalde are just a few examples of these. The domestic pig (Schwein) takes second place, way behind, with 105 towns that have names connected with it, such as Schweinfurt or Schweinheim.

But Germany is not the only country to have used the bear in designing coats of arms or flags over the past centuries. The official coats of arms for the Swiss cities of Bern and St. Gallen, for example, are also embellished by wonderful bear images.

FROM FAIRYTALE CHARACTER TO TOY ANIMAL

Bears often also feature as the leading figures in fairytales, myths and fables from all over the world. The most well-known of these must be the story of "Snow White and Rose Red" by the Brothers Grimm that was published in 1812. This is the story of an enchanted prince who has to maintain his silence in the form of a bear. The spell is finally broken with the death of the evil dwarf who put the curse on him and he can then marry Snow White.

Another fairytale published during the same year tells the story of a man who seals a pact with the devil and, as a result, has to wear a bear-skin for seven years.

Fig. 172: Unjointed bear dating back to the pre-Teddy era.

The bear's powers of attraction for mankind are just as indisputable today as they have been for thousands of years. It is therefore hardly surprising to discover that there were many other toys modelled on the bear and made of the most diverse materials well before the Teddy bear appeared on the scene. Mechanical bears with muzzles existed in France, for example, as early as the 19th century. There are also records of very early toys in the form of bears in Russia. Some of the famous Dymkovo clay toys were modelled on bears. Toy bears made of wood and the Steiff bears from the early years provide further evidence of this.

All of the early toy bears were made of hard materials, however, and resembled the natural creatures that they were modelled on very closely in terms of both proportions and facial expression.

The re-emergence of humanism in the 18th/19th centuries signals a change in people's attitude to toys: for the first time, childhood is regarded as being an important stage in the development of a human being. Education assumes a significant role and importance is attached to learning. Children are no longer regarded as being imperfect adults, or even useless eaters who do nothing to earn their daily bread. They are allowed to be what they are: young people to be escorted along the road to adulthood. Children are finally permitted to act their age and can enjoy playing, being silly and showing their emotions.

At time passes, the prevailing standard of living gradually makes it possible for the majority of people to think of more pleasant things than simply surviving from one day to the next.

Increasing prosperity enables people to afford things and treat themselves. And these include buying pretty toys for the children – plush animals, for instance. Toys acquire a completely new status. Toys can be used to simply pass the time or to provide support for teaching and educational purposes. Children can play through situations in our day-to-day routines and, at the same time, prepare themselves for tasks and duties in their adult lives.

Already very popular, even at this time, dolls assume an important role for little girls: these little images of human beings offer them a means of learning to take care of others, assume responsibility and express such emotions as love or anger. However, the allocation of male and female roles at that time would not permit little boys to play with dolls.

Fig. 173: Snow White, Rose Red and the bear – a limited edition of 1200 sets comprising the two dolls and the bear – manufactured by Steiff in 1992.

The Teddy bear therefore arrived on the scene just in time in 1902. Richard Steiff may possibly even have been primarily concerned with finding a toy for little boys – a counterpart for the doll.

Be that as it may: a proper little boy had to have a proper bear. The son and heir could at last establish an intimate relationship with a toy without being regarded as a weakling or an object of ridicule. Nowadays, we know how important it is for children to have 'someone' else to relate to apart from their parents, someone with whom they can share secrets, large and small, and confide their worries and desires: a true and loyal friend, who always listens with a sympathetic ear, never argues and keeps every secret, is just what's needed.

Whatever a child's imagination demands of Teddy, he is always ready to slip into the required role. He can be the most courageous warrior of them all, invincible and feared by everyone and, a few seconds later, the embarrassed schoolboy who's forgotten his homework or is standing in front of the blackboard and doesn't know what to do next. Teddy never umbrage at being the target for aggressive behaviour, nor does mind being the subject of any injustices. He never bears a grudge, is always there when needed and will always remain a sympathetic friend. He was therefore not only loved by little boys, but also found his way into the hearts of little girls and many adults.

Fig. 174: Something for everyone – Steiff's "Goldilocks" set unites doll and bears.

Fig. 175: Steiff bear from the "Goldilocks" set.

THE TEDDY AS A TRUE LIFETIME COMPANION

One can snuggle and cuddle up to a Teddy, which is something one can't do with a doll that doesn't have the bear's beautiful, soft fur coat. And even the greatest cares can often be forgotten when he starts growling with pleasure.

Teddy bears received in the cradle therefore accompany innumerable people all through their lives. Teddy still has his age-old fascination even today in this age of excess stimulation.

Every person's Teddy bear has its own very special significance that changes with the passage of time. Contact with the soft fur is simply pleasant and cosy for an infant. Teddy doesn't become Teddy until a children is a little older. As the years pass, he puts his almost unlimited talents as a friend and comforter, listener, teacher and analyst to use – an undemanding playmate and lifetime companion in every situation.

Fig. 176: The Teddy bear – equally
popular among boys and girls.

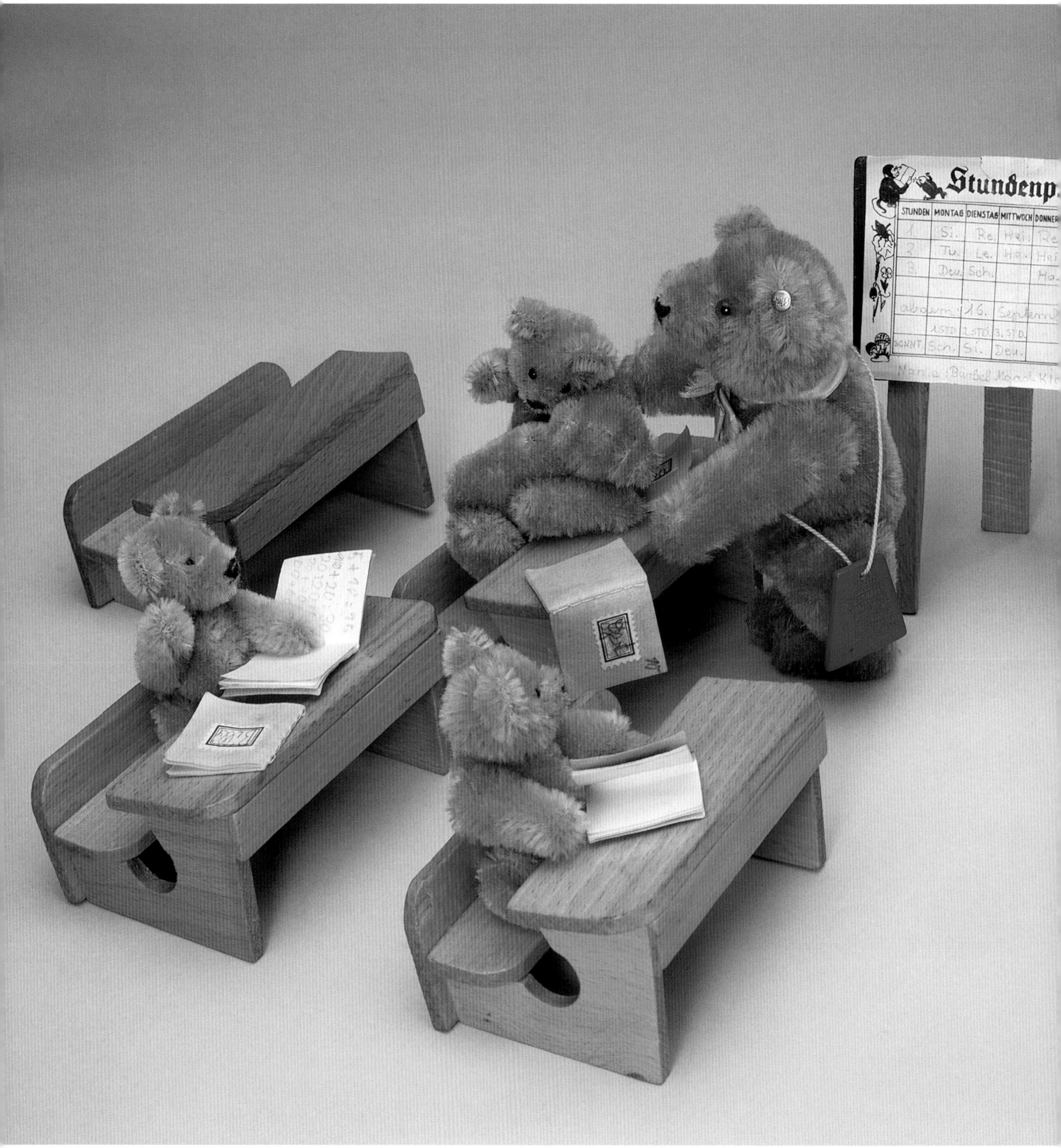
STUNDEN
MONTAG
DIENSTAG
MITTWOCH

Fig. 178: The Teddy bear – a faithful friend, not just during childhood years.

Fig. 179: Teddy as a "lucky charm" from the current Steiff Collection.

Fig. 177: Courageous warrior or embarrassed schoolboy, Teddy plays every role assigned to him perfectly.

Taken on journeys, he is usually given a place of honour, from where he can keep an eye on everything and is always close at hand should the need arise. A child interprets all affection bestowed on Teddy by his or her parents as indications of their affection for him or her. The child's social conduct is moulded and a feeling of belonging develops that can make a considerable contribution towards a childhood being happy and harmonious.

Teddy usually moves into an unassuming position in the background during the teens. There is often little room for a faithful companion from the past during the growing-up phase when the up-and-coming adult breaks with childhood habits. Teddy will be given a place on the bookshelf if he is lucky. Less fortunate bears are crammed into boxes with other toys and end up in the attic.

Experience has shown that, once the teenager has grown into an adult and life has moved into calmer waters, happy memories of the loyal childhood friend are enjoyed again. And, as years go by and people get older, they spend more and more time thinking about the past. The Teddy bear frequently becomes a symbol for long-forgotten experiences, dreams and wishes. Even if he isn't really alive, the memories associated with Teddy do seem to breathe life into him to a certain extent.

Some families have already adopted a tradition of handing Teddy bears down from one generation to the next. As a result, there are one or two Teddy bears that have already seen and experienced so many things that they have become parts of history themselves. Old or new, toy or collector's item, mascot or lucky charm – there will always be a place for Teddy bears in this world as long as the human race continues to exist.

Collectors' Tales

WHY DO PEOPLE ACTUALLY COLLECT STEIFF TEDDY BEARS? SELECTED CONNOISSEURS TELL THEIR STORIES AND DESCRIBE THE REASONS THAT MADE THEM DECIDE ON STEIFF ANIMALS AS THE SUBJECT OF THEIR HOBBY.

Fig. 180: Toys of yesteryear –
collectors' treasures of today.

More than 100,000 people all over the world collect the Steiff animals that have been manufactured in Giengen an der Brenz for over 120 years now. The roads that led them there are just as multifarious as the reasons why they pursue their passion for collecting.

Some particularly impressive examples are portrayed below:

Steiff collectors, whose daily lives are in the public eye and who therefore tend to pursue their hobby discretely in the background, reveal their reasons for collecting Steiff animals.

PROFESSOR JÜRGEN HUBBERT
AND HIS MOST FAITHFUL COMPANION

Professor Jürgen Hubbert is one example. He has occupied one of the world's most responsible management positions for many years now in his capacity as a member of the Management Board of DaimlerChrysler AG.

His face is no longer unfamiliar thanks to his frequent appearances in the box of the McLaren Mercedes Formula 1 team and the associated reports broadcast by virtually every TV station in the world.

What is it about Steiff animals that makes a busy company boss of such high standing collect them rather than model cars, toys made of tin plate or works of art?

He answers this question spontaneously and without beating about the bush: born in Hagen, Westphalia, in 1939, Mr. Hubbert was forced to leave not one, but two completely bombed-out houses as a very young child during the 2nd World War. The only toy that survived with him was his one faithful companion, a white Steiff Teddy, around 25 cm tall. And this very Teddy bear means a great deal more to Professor Hubbert today than just being the central figure of his collection. That is clearly apparent when we actually get a glimpse of the bear in question. Speaking firmly with one hundred percent self-possession and without a trace of sentimentality, Mr. Hubbert tells us that this bear has been his constant companion throughout his lifetime and that there is no reason why this should change in the event of his death. Just the thought of his little bear being put on show as an attraction in a museum or becoming part of an eminent collection is completely out of the question for the long-standing collector.

The natural, matter-of-fact and precise manner in which this sophisticated man describes his emotional relationship with his Teddy bear is remarkably impressive. In spite of the sympathetic sensitivity that he expresses here, I certainly don't get the impression that the man in front is a dreamy romantic, not for a second.

Quite the contrary: In the subsequent photo session the manager follows the photographer's instructions with utmost professionalism. There is not a trace of insecurity in the way in which he allows himself to be photographed with and without his

Figs. 181/182: Professor Jürgen Hubbert and his Teddy bear.

Teddy bear – a man who knows exactly what he is doing in every phase of his life and can therefore stand by everything that he does in a natural, unaffected way.

It isn't difficult to give unreserved credence to his words when he says that he only collects Steiff animals because he likes them and because he feels a special affinity with these large and small masterpieces. Jürgen Hubbert's enthusiasm is substantiated by a tour of the room specially furnished to accommodate his Steiff collection. Creatures of virtually every type are carefully arranged in glass cases – different bears and Teddy bears, felt dolls, glove puppets, woollen miniatures and many other articles from the many-facetted Steiff product spectrum. Wonderful exhibits from the early days juxtaposed with articles from the current Steiff collection, as well as play-worn items next to exhibits preserved in mint condition. Everything looks very well cared-for and it's obvious that this collection has been lovingly built up over many years.

Incidentally, Steiff products constitute the sole subject of Mr. Hubbert's "collectivitis". The white Teddy was occasionally joined by a new Steiff animal as early as 1959, when he started studying in Stuttgart. Having started up the career ladder and marrying his wife in 1965, he gradually became increasingly involved in his hobby to such an extent that he became a regular visitor at the flea markets that he had only attended from time to time before 1970. By the way, Mrs. Hubbert also collects dolls with the same dedication that her husband devotes to his Steiff articles – an ideal partnership, there's no doubt about that.

Nowadays, when Mr. Hubbert visits flea markets, toy collectors' markets or auctions, he always has to think up something new in order to avoid being recognised as soon as he arrives. But, even as he talks about his attempts to disguise himself, it is clearly evident that he enjoys everything about his hobby and what it involves, and wouldn't give it up for the world. The same applies to his refusal to deviate from the hard and fast rules that he has set himself when it comes to the price of a new collector's item. He always keeps within his self-imposed top price limit. Even if one particular treasure really appeals to him: Professor Hubbert is quite capable of saying "no" if asked to pay an excessively high price. His many years of collecting experience has taught him that there will probably be a second chance. And knowing exactly what he wants has become routine for him during his many years in a top executive position.

It all began more than 60 years ago with the white Steiff Teddy bear that is the only surviving companion from Jürgen Hubbert's earliest childhood years. This Teddy still has a permanent place at the side of his proud owner – and it looks as though he is going to stay there for ever.

GIGI OERI AND HER UNIQUE, DECORATIVE EXHIBITS

Our next journey takes us to Switzerland, where more than 30 museums within an area of just 37 square kilometres attract visitors to the cultural city of Basle. And one of these museums is where we are aiming for: the doll's house museum.

Known as "Gigi", Gisela Oeri came up with the idea in 1996. What she managed to achieve in the little more than 24 months leading up to the museum's official opening

Fig. 183: The doll's house museum – right in the heart of Basle.

Fig. 184: Gigi Oeri in front of a showcase containing Steiff Teddy bears in the doll's house museum.

in 1998 is quite extraordinary: the house situated at Steinenvorstadt No. 1 in Basle was completely renovated and refurbished according to the special requirements of a museum, right down to the very last detail. At the same time, bears and dolls were added to Gigi Oeri's collection, which had predominantly consisted of precious doll's houses up to then. Unique and unparalleled in terms of variety, perfection and delightful arrangements anywhere in the world, the resulting exhibition of Steiff bears is a tribute to her dedication.

In the few years that have past since it opened, the doll's house museum has become world-famous under the management of Ms. Oeri, thanks to its valuable and unique exhibits.

Only very few visitors are aware, however, that each and every one of the items on display in this wonderful museum is the personal property of the initiator and therefore belong to Gigi Oeri's personal collection.

Having studied sport and worked as a physiotherapist, she was gripped by "collectivitis" at the age of 25. She fell for some miniatures that were on show at the Basle Autumn Fair. In the words of welcome that Ms. Oeri has written in the museum guide, she says: "Fascinated by the variety offered by the stands and the hustle and bustle all around, I came up with the idea of reproducing the scene on a scale of 1:12 and capturing a little bit of the very special atmosphere that prevailed in the Petersplatz. I spent countless hours sawing, gluing, moulding and painting until a familiar, but newly created inside landscape materialised in front of me, stand by stand." There is really no better way to describe the enthusiasm and true motives that led to the subsequent expansion of Gigi Oeri's collection.

As the years passed, the miniatures that she had made herself were joined by an antique carousel, the most exquisite doll's houses, toy grocer's shops and many other treasures.

Steiff bears were not included in the collection until the decision to open the museum in Basle had been made. The energy and vitality that helped Gigi Oeri to gather such an incredible collection of the most rare and beautiful Steiff bears around her within less than 2 years become clearly evident as she describes the details of the events as they happened.

The constant stream of new challenges presented by developing arrangements that are even more beautiful and closer to her ideal keeps her hobby alive and makes it so attractive to her. And new, previously undreamt-of dimensions of creativity opened up for Gigi Oeri when she started adding other Steiff products to her collection. After all, she didn't stop at just Steiff bears: a multitude of other Steiff animals have now found their places in the Oeri collection and have taken up residence in the doll's house museum. And she admits that another love of her life was kindled during her last visit to the archives of Margarete Steiff GmbH. That was when she laid eyes on the wonderful Steiff felt dolls from the early days. It will be exciting to see what other treasures will be unearthed by Gigi Oeri in the future and we can look forward to some interesting surprises.

Although Ms. Oeri's collection was initially focussed on the miniatures, Steiff Teddy bears now occupy the main focal point in her collection. As far as she is

Fig. 185: Steiff felt doll "Peary 43" from the Steiff archive, manufactured between 1909 and 1910 and named after polar explorer Robert Edwin Peary.

Fig. 186: Wilhelm Busch's Max and Moritz were included in the Steiff product range between 1910 and 1926. The felt dolls produced by Margarete Steiff GmbH follow a great tradition. Looking at these wonderful examples, it is easy to understand the enthusiasm that has also captured Gigi Oeri now.

concerned, Steiff is the Rolls Royce among toy manufacturers. She is fascinated by the history of the company as well as its products. But Gigi Oeri is most enthusiastic about the infinite creative possibilities offered to her by the products of more than 120 years of company history, as she was at the beginning of her collecting activities.

A lady who needs a constant stream of new challenges but never loses interest or élan in a project once started. Standstill is a word that she's never heard of, but what Ms. Oeri is looking for is not found in short-lived successes. When she decides to take something on, she does so with conviction, enthusiasm and one hundred percent commitment. And this conviction and enthusiasm is not just devoted to her hobbies, she also adopts the same attitude in pursuing her objectives in every situation.

One thing that demands special respect is that Gigi Oeri allows all of her friends and collectors from all over the world, in particular, to share the enjoyment of her "collectivitis". It is worth visiting the doll's house museum again and again to take advantage of the opportunity to examine the treasures that have been united in her collection.

Fig. 187: Frankfurt, the centre of European banking.

THOMAS LO – STEIFF ANIMALS AS AN ENDEARING INVESTMENT

Having left Switzerland, we now return to Germany. To Frankfurt am Main, the home of Hesse's State Central Bank. We are visiting Thomas Lo, one of the directors of the Federal Bank, head of the legal department and co-publisher of a loose-leaf reference work on European Economic Law.

Asked about the reason for his collecting inclination, Mr. Lo doesn't beat about the bush and simply explains that, apart from the capital investments that are customary in his business, he has also been investing money in his toy collections over the past 20 years. In the plush toy sector, his attention is exclusively concentrated on products from the most reputable German company with the greatest tradition – Margarete Steiff GmbH.

I must admit to being a little surprised to hear that such an experienced bank manager refers to capital investments when answering this question and, wanting to find out more, I ask Mr. Lo for a more detailed explanation. He promptly responds to my question with a question of his own: "What do Peck, a promotion figure manufactured for Merck by Steiff in the 1950s, an Oezipek silk carpet with almost 2.5 million knots per square metre, a Schuco model car produced for the 2001 New York Toy Fair and an Eiswein (a sweet German wine made from frost bitten grapes) with almost 200 degrees "Oechsle" (a measure of its potential alcohol content), have in common? – All of these are rare, much sought-after collector's items, that embody an exceptional standard of quality as a result of their origins and manufacture as top-class products of their respective species. Apart from that, they are usually made by hand and produced in limited quantities. Unlike common-or-garden mass-produced goods, these articles are good value for money in the truest sense of the term, i.e. they are really worth the value paid for them. This means that their value not only remains stable, but can also be expected to increase considerably. And while money and securities just

Fig. 188: The premises of Hesse's State Central Bank in Frankfurt/Main – the current business address of Federal Bank Director Thomas Lo.

Fig. 189: Thomas Lo, Director of the Federal Bank

appear in the form of figures on bank statements, collectors' items and works of art also offer a means of decorating the home and give pleasure to their collector every day."

Thomas Lo's story opened with a newspaper article about Steiff bears. It reported about a Teddy bear that was no longer available on the market.

In his working life, lawyer Thomas Lo is used to solving difficult problems successfully, even if this involves a great deal of expense and stress. He also enjoys setting himself ambitious, challenging targets in his free time. The prospect of getting hold of the Teddy that, according to the press report, was no longer available therefore held a particular appeal for him. As chance would have it, the allegedly almost impossible task proved to be relatively easy – he took possession of the Teddy bear just a short time later. But this easily solved "case" was not to be the last, as Mr. Lo likes to get to the bottom of things in his private life, as well as in his day-to-day business routine.

He began to gather detailed information about the market for Steiff collectors, which was still fairly straightforward at that time. He initially concentrated on the series of Steiff replicas, that began with the so-called "Papa bear" in 1980. He soon developed a feeling for the Steiff models with special appreciation potential because of their rarity or peculiarity, or simply because of their exceptional natural beauty.

Mr. Lo has not sold any of the articles that he has collected up to now. Nevertheless, he is particularly delighted when comparable collectors' items fetch prices that represent several hundred percent appreciation on their original selling prices at auction. As Mr. Lo admits without hesitation: "Such sudden increases in profits are seldom found even in financial markets" – and one thing becomes immediately obvious: The Federal Bank Director knows what he's talking about.

Thomas Lo is firmly convinced that the name and products of the Steiff company will continue to be linked with the terms "tradition, quality and value" in the future and that the international interest of collectors and investors will increase to a greater extent in the years to come.

When the time is right, the Federal Bank Director intends to donate his toy collection to the Salzburg Seminar and set up a toy museum in its baroque home – Leopoldskron Castle, which was used in the well-known American musical film "The Sound of Music". The Salzburg Seminar is a global organisation, composed of leading figures from the worlds of business, art, culture and science, which means that this would be the ideal place to make the valuable top-class products of German toy manufacturers accessible to international guests as an expression of national tradition and culture.

Until this happens, Thomas Lo is quite happy to use his Steiff animals for their original purpose: as extremely popular toys for the children of his friends, most of whom come from abroad. Completely in accordance with the "Friends for Life" motto that is so important to international understanding.

Fig. 190: Steiff produced Peck Greenfly, also known as the "cough goblin", as a promotion article for Merck in Darmstadt during the 1950s. Collectors are already willing to pay more than US$ 2,500 for a well-preserved example today.

118

Fig. 191: Known as
"Papa bear", this was
the first reproduction of an old bear manufactured by Steiff
in 1980 and heralded the beginning of the Steiff replicas
which have become very popular all over the world.

IAN POUT – FROM STOCK BROKER TO ANTIQUE COLLECTOR

Our next station is England, where we meet one of the pioneers among Steiff collectors. Ian Pout earned his daily bread as a stock broker up to 1973. The Middle East conflict that was prevailing at the time, and the oil shortage that also affected his business transactions, contributed towards taking the fun out his working life. The daily ups and downs began to get on his nerves. Without further ado, he decided to turn his hobby into a career after discussing the matter with his wife. Mr. Pout became an antique dealer. He moved into the country with his wife and devoted his entire attention to the new task.

He hasn't regretted this decision up to now. Although setting up the new business was a very time-consuming process, Ian enjoyed having his family close at hand – with the offspring that had arrived in the meantime – and no longer being exposed to the stress of the stock market day in day out. He never doubted his decision, not even for a second, in spite of the greater financial opportunities offered by his old job.

Fig. 192: Ian Pout in front of his Teddy shop "Teddy Bears of Witney" in Oxfordshire.

120

Fig. 193: Alfonzo with the family tree of the Russian tsarist family, the family of his original owner.

As far as the antiques are concerned, Ian Pout is particularly fond of those items that tell their own verifiable stories. He is always fascinated by the fact that he can almost live through past events himself when delving into the history behind some of the old treasures. Although older bears were occasionally offered to him, he didn't really know what to do with them when he first started up in the antique business.

Not long afterwards, he first heard of Colonel Bob Henderson, the enthusiastic bear collector and founder of the English "Good Bears of the World" organisation, and Peter Bull, the English character actor, who has even written several books about

Fig. 195: Ian Pout bought Alfonzo, Princess Xenia's bear at auction in May 1989 for around US$ 20,400, an exceptionally high price at the time.

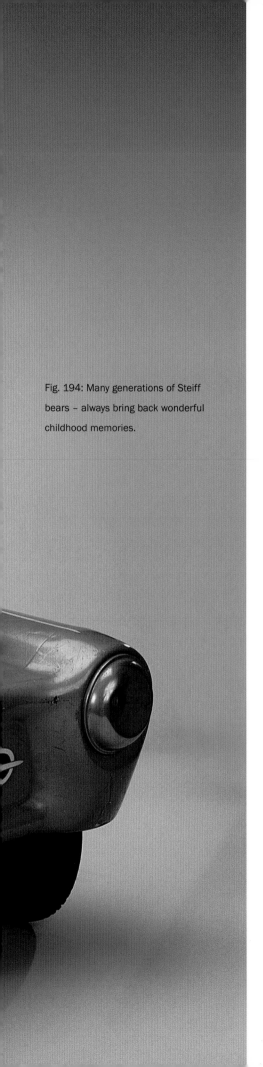

Fig. 194: Many generations of Steiff bears – always bring back wonderful childhood memories.

Teddy bears. It was with this inspiration that Ian Pout began collecting Teddy bears at the beginning of the 1980s. 1985 saw him already opening one of the first bear shops in Oxfordshire under the name "Teddy Bears of Witney". The product range comprises a successful combination of old and new Teddies. Articles from his own collection are exhibited in special showcases and the items offered for sale include bears from currently produced collections, as well as veteran bears of all shapes and sizes.

Ian Pout's ears pricked up in May 1989 when a very special bear was put up for auction at Christie's in London. "Alfonzo", the red Steiff bear belonging to Princess Xenia of Russia, the great-great-granddaughter of Catherine the Great. Xenia was given this bear in 1908 as a gift from her father, George Michailovitch, Grand Prince of Russia. She was in England during the Russian Revolution and survived. Shortly afterwards, Xenia emigrated to America with Alfonzo and her husband William Leeds, living in Long Island until her death in 1965.

Just 33 cm tall, this bear could relate the entire history of the tsarist family and that was just the thing for Ian Pout. After battling with many international bidders, the hammer finally fell in his favour at £ 12,100 (approximately US$ 20,400), a fantastic price at the time.

Fig. 196: Ian Pout and his "Teddy Bears of Witney" are always in attendance at the annual Steiff Festival in Giengen.

Fig. 197: Theodore, English actor Peter Bull's acknowledged favourite bear.

Fig. 198: Colonel
Bob Henderson and
his "Teddy Girl".

From today's standpoint, paying such a high price for a Teddy bear in 1989 was a really revolutionary thing to do. But as far as Ian Pout is concerned, this bear is still "worth more than any other bear in the world because it is so rare and tells such a romantic story". And he proved to be right. If Alfonzo were to be sold today, the price that he would fetch would be several times higher than the original amount paid. This bear is not for sale, however, and has now become the trademark of the world famous bear shop in Oxfordshire. Ian has been able to acquire quite a few other bears with histories since then.

Colonel Bob Henderson's famous collection was put up for auction on December 5th, 1994. It included probably the oldest bear in England: a Steiff "Bärle", 46 cm tall, that was manufactured in 1905. The English bear enthusiast was still hoping to keep this bear in England right up to the last minute, but had to admit defeat in the end when the bear was sold to the highest bidder from Japan. "Teddy Girl", as his former owner affectionately called her, changed hands for £ 110,000 including fees (more than US$ 120,000).

But a new opportunity came up just a year later, on December 11th, 1995, when "Theodore", Peter Bull's most faithful companion, was auctioned. Just 10 cm tall, this little bear had become just as famous as his former owner as a result of his appearances in numerous books and, above all, the fact that he always accompanied the well-known actor on his travels all over the world.

Dating back to 1948, this little chap fetched £ 14,300 (approximately US$ 22,000). Like Alfonzo, Theodore is now regarded as being one of the main attractions in the exhibition of Ian Pout's private collection, which can still be admired in his shop "Teddy Bears of Witney".

Fig. 199: Cuddly dreams made of
plush – a delight for any collector.

Four enthusiastic Steiff collectors with completely different roads leading them to their "collectivitis" and different motives that have induced them to remain faithful to their hobby over so many years.

All of these stories have one thing in common, however, and this is something that they share with every single member of the steadily growing collecting community: they love the articles produced by Steiff and are happy to let themselves be taken down memory lane to revisit their childhood days over and over again.

The Teddy Bear as an Antique and Collector's Item

IX.

ABOUT PRECIOUS ANTIQUES

AND VALUABLE COLLECTOR'S ITEMS –

TEDDY BEARS AND OTHER TOY ANIMALS

FROM THE STEIFF COMPANY ...

Fig. 200: A rare sight that makes every collector's heart beat just that little bit faster.

Fig. 201: Steiff collectors
can pursue their hobby in so
many different ways.

Going back to man's early history, our forefathers instinctively busied themselves as hunters and gatherers to meet their daily needs with what nature had to offer. As loners or in convenient groups, most of man's time was spent searching for food, clothing or accommodation, activities that could be extremely dangerous under certain circumstances. Law and order were regulated according to the rules of the strongest. A great deal has changed since then, thank heavens. Nowadays, man's social existence is organised according to guidelines and directives, our fundamental rights are assured by constitutions and there are authorities who ensure compliance with these rules. The time that an individual needs to safeguard his existence and earn his daily bread is decreasing continuously. We are now living in a leisure society and use the increasing amount of free time that is available in very different ways. The most varied kinds of sport, as active participant or spectator, holidays to suit every taste, travelling to the furthest corners of the world and even to the moon, games for outside and indoors, handicrafts, reading and making or listening to music – there is virtually no end to the range of possible leisure activities that are available. In the meantime, whole industrial sectors have been established to ensure that nobody gets bored.

Fig. 202: Bear 28PB from 1905 and
Jackie from 1953 – two stars in every
bear collector's heaven.

COLLECTING AS THE MOST POPULAR PASTIME

Collecting things is and always will be one of the most attractive and diversified leisure-time activities. It is debatable whether hereditary factors are responsible for this or not. It is a fact, however, that more than half of the people interviewed in relevant surveys said that collecting is one of their favourite hobbies. The motives leading to this hobby-horse are manifold. And the objects collected by people today are just as multifarious. From simple beer mats through to expensive works of art, there is virtually nothing that is not worth collecting.

Collections are sometimes initiated as the result of highly topical, cleverly market-ed fashion trends, which die down again as quickly as they started. This can frequently be a painful experience for the collectors concerned. Forced upwards to

Fig. 203: The creative options available to Steiff collectors are virtually endless.

astronomical heights, the artificial price level bursts like a bubble and suddenly nobody shows any further interest in the apparently so sought-after collector's items of yesterday. Pleasure and enthusiasm soon die away when the entire market collapses almost overnight. Anyone wishing to avoid such unpleasant experiences should consider and review various factors before deciding on a specific subject area for his or her collection.

It goes without saying that the objects under consideration must be things that please and interest the potential collector. The amount of space required to accommodate the collection must be taken into account, and the collector must ensure that his or her financial possibilities are in harmony with the planned investments.

Fig. 204: Disney articles from
the current Steiff range

Fig. 205: ... or what about the
Mickey Mouse from the 1930s?

Anyone wishing to choose a field that is likely to survive the passage of time rather than being a short-lived trend can either restrict the choice to such established subjects as coins, stamps, china, antiques or works of art, for example. If these seem too boring or the potential collector has other interests, he or she should ensure that at least the following criteria are taken into consideration: expertise and specialist knowledge are fundamental prerequisites, which is why it is particularly important to gather comprehensive information about the hobby before buying the first item. Although subject-specific literature and discussions with experienced collectors make it easier to get started, personal experience can only be built up over years of constant, intensive involvement with the articles. As far as more recent collector's items are concerned, it is important to ensure that there is a good price-performance ratio, i.e. that the manufacturing costs are in accordance with the quality of the article. Other rules apply, of course, if there is already a secondary market for the selected articles. In this case, the prices are determined by the free-market principles of supply and demand. Prices can then be compared with those fetched at auction or the prices asked by reputable dealers.

There's not much that can go wrong if these guidelines are followed and the newly fledged collector will soon be able to enjoy the fun of his or her new-found hobby to the full.

A VERY SPECIAL COLLECTORS' SECTOR: STEIFF TEDDY BEARS AND TOY ANIMALS

The collector who decides to focus on Teddy bears and animals made by Steiff can be sure that he or she has chosen one of the most wonderful and enticing subjects of the collecting world. The products manufactured in Giengen ceased to be solely destined for children's hands many years ago. A continuously growing community of collectors and enthusiasts has built up all over the world. When Steiff animals appeared in the world's most renowned auction rooms, this finally signalled their successful breakthrough to becoming acknowledged collectors' items.

Collectors can choose from products manufactured over more than 120 years of company history. Precious antiques, valuable collectors' pieces or the latest additions to the extensive current Steiff product range fulfil nearly every collector's heart-felt dreams. An almost inexhaustible range of wonderful Steiff products are available from reputable toy shops and the Steiff Galleries, as well as special collectors' shops, markets and auctions. Young or old, lady or gentleman – there's something to suit every taste and pocket.

Fig. 206: The currently most expensive Teddy bear in the world fetched more than US$ 130,000 at auction on December 4th, 2000.

Fig. 208: Bear 28PB, who changed hands at the special auction held within the framework of the Steiff Festival in Giengen for almost US$ 120,000, dates back to 1904.

Fig. 207: The Steiff Club is also available to its members at the annual Steiff Festival.

Excellent reading matter is also available, as well as opportunities to exchange opinions and experiences with other collectors. Founded in 1992, the Steiff Club has already attracted more than 50,000 members worldwide – enthusiasts and collectors of the articles from Giengen – and there are new members joining every day.

NOT ONLY COLLECTORS ARE IMPRESSED BY REMARKABLE AUCTION RESULTS

The world's most renowned auction houses now offer special auctions just for Steiff animals. The record figures fetched here continue to surpass themselves. The world's currently most expensive Teddy bear was sold at Christie's in London on December 4th, 2000, when the hammer fell at around £ 91,750 including charges (more than US$ 130,000). He is 50 cm tall and dates back to 1912 as part of a special series of black mohair Teddy bears made when the Titanic went down. In the same year, on July 1st, 2000, a bear 28PB, that was manufactured in 1904 was sold at the special auction organised by GAF Günther Pfeiffer GmbH within

133

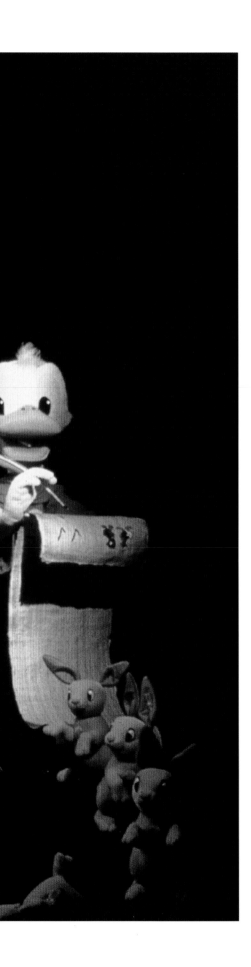

the framework of the Steiff Festival in Giengen, for almost US$ 120,000 (including charges).

The list of record figures for 2000 would not be complete without the article that fetched more than US$ 100,000 at Sotheby's. Made specially for Disney, a Steiff showpiece depicting Noah's Ark went under the hammer in New York on June 29th, 2000, for US$ 110,000 (including charges).

It is therefore not only the Teddy bears from Steiff that sell for such extraordinarily high figures. Two other recent examples are the little elephant "Elefäntle" and a clothed Peter Rabbit. The Elefäntle, a pin cushion in the form of an elephant, was the first plush animal ever made by Margarete Steiff. The "Elefäntle" that was sold at the special auction held during the Steiff Festival in Giengen on July 1st, 2000, was just 8 cm tall and dates back to 1893. Fetching almost US$ 23,000, that was the highest price ever paid for a Steiff animal at the time (not including Teddy bears). This record was broken just a year later, however, during the next Festival auction. Wearing a felt jacket and slippers, Steiff's Peter Rabbit was sold for more than US$ 29,000 and snatched the title of most expensive Steiff animal away from the "Elefäntle".

Fig. 209: The Steiff showpiece depicting Noah's Ark for Disney was auctioned for US$ 110,000 in New York in the year 2000.

Fig. 210: Made of wool plush, the white Peter Rabbit was manufactured around 1904/05 and went under the hammer for more than US$ 29,000 in 2001.

Fig. 211: A record price of almost US$ 23,000 was paid for the Steiff "Elefäntle" on July 1st, 2000.

Fig. 212: "Teddy Peace",
a predecessor of the Teddy clown fetched
more than US$ 108,000 in 1997.

Fig. 213: "Teddy Girl" was sold for the record price of more than US$ 120,000 on December 5th, 1994.

Fig. 214: Just 10 cm tall, this little 1950s Steiff bear was sold for more than US$ 24,000 on June 30th, 2001.

The prices fetched by Teddy bears at auction are somewhat higher. A record price was paid for the "Teddy Girl" from Colonel Bob Henderson's collection mentioned in an earlier chapter as early as 1994. On December 5th, 1994, the 46 cm Steiff "Bärle" from 1905 was auctioned at Christie's in London for a total of £ 110,000 including charges (more than US$ 120,000).

The top prices paid for the next two Teddy bears were again achieved at the special auctions in Giengen organised by GAF Günther Pfeiffer GmbH. On July 5th, 1997, more than US$ 108,000 was paid for a brown tipped Teddy bear dating back to 1925, a predecessor of the Teddy clown. This bear has now taken up residence in a Teddy museum in Japan and his new owners have affectionately renamed him "Teddy Peace".

Two years later, it was Harlekin (refer to page 139), the 35 cm Teddy made of red and blue mohair, who caused the next sensation on June 19th, 1999. After fierce bidding, the hammer finally fell on this unique bear from the colourful 1920s period at more than US$ 95,000.

The list of Steiff articles that have fetched prices well in excess of US$ 50,000 at auctions could go on for quite a while. But let us bring it to a close by mentioning one last very special record: the smallest bear and the only one produced during the period following the 2nd World War to fetch such a high price – a little black Steiff bear, just ten centimetres tall, dating back to the 1950s. It was sold for more than US$ 24,000 at the auction held during the Steiff Festival in Giengen on June 30th, 2001. A truly fantastic price for such a tiny fellow.

Fig. 215: The record-breakers are certainly not the only articles with bear appeal – these Steiff bears dating back to the period between 1925 and 1940 have their own very special charm, in spite of being play-worn and by no means perfect, they are also regarded as being treasures by most collectors.

The £ 12,100 (around US$ 20,400) paid for "Alfonzo" in 1989 seems almost modest by comparison (refer to Chapter VIII). The record price for a Teddy bear increased by 1000 percent in just eleven years – from 1989 to 2000 – which implies that several surprises will be waiting for us in the years ahead.

A comparison with other collectibles also indicates favourable prospects for the increasing prices of Steiff Teddies and other animals to be expected in the future. The top prices paid for stamps, for example, left the million euro mark behind some time ago. However, postage stamps have been collected for a hundred years already, which dates the first collection at around the time that Richard Steiff created the very first jointed bear. If the records continue to be broken with the same regularity as they have been in recent years, it doesn't look as though we shall have to wait very long before comparable results are achieved.

Fig. 216: Record prices for Steiff Teddies and animals are usually achieved within the framework of auctions – this one was held during the Steiff Festival in Giengen.

All of these records only account for a very small, albeit very important element of the collector's world. And, although the sensational headlines take care of the public relations work that is essential to even the most beautiful product, the real appeal is radiated by the countless treasures, large and small, that are kept in the many private collections and give renewed pleasure and enjoyment to their owners every day.

Fig. 217: "Harlekin" is the most colourful
Steiff bear of them all. He was sold at auction for
more than US$ 95,000 on June 19th, 1999.

100 Years of Teddy Bear Models

MANY DIFFERENT VERSIONS FOLLOWED
IN THE STEPS OF THE FIRST JOINTED BEAR –
TEDDY BEAR MODELS INTRODUCE
THEMSELVES ...

Fig. 218: An age difference of almost
90 years between the Bear 28PB
dating back to 1904 and the Original
Teddy bear produced in 1991.

Fig. 219: The bear ladder was included in the Steiff product range for many years and has now become a much sought-after display article.

I t goes without saying that the Teddy bear has gone through a lot of changes over the last 100 years – both external and internal. And there are various factors that have contributed towards this. The changes that took place during the early years were primarily due to the development of the design: Richard Steiff – like his successors – never grew tired of varying the quality and appearance of the bears and adapting them to suit the style of the time. The fixing technique used to secure the head and limbs was developed further, for example, new stuffing materials were tested, growlers were introduced and patterns modified.

The Teddy bear has to keep abreast with the fashions whether he wants to or not. The rules are by no means as strict as those that apply to the fashions presented on the catwalks, of course. But it is not always just minor details that are altered with respect to the pattern, the features or the accessories.

The famous Teddy hump, for example, diminishes from decade to decade, until it finally disappears completely. Arms and legs become shorter, the ears gradually creep upwards towards the top of the head and completely new materials are even used for the nose and eyes. Muzzle or bathing suit, clown costume or wedding dress, the Teddy wears and bears everything with his own, inherent patience.

In economically or politically difficult times, when the mohair plush that had become standard material for the Teddy bear was not available, the people at Steiff created their own substitutes in order to be able to continue production of the animal that had become a firm favourite for people of all ages. One of these was a sort

Fig. 220: A "motley" crowd
of Teddy bears dating back to
between 1905 and 1940.

of cellulose material produced from wood fibre that was used to make what became known as the "paper Teddy" shortly after the 1st World War. During the 2nd World War, Teddy bears were produced using synthetic silk plush until 1949, when production could be resumed with the tried-and-trusted mohair.

Only a selection of the many different models that were issued as Steiff Teddy bears over the last 100 years are presented in the summary that follows. Even if all of the important and interesting designs and variations are described in detail, this summary by no means claims to be complete – that would go way beyond the scope of this book.

Fig. 221: Bear 28PB

and Bear 35PB

The bears were measured sitting down from 1904 onwards. According to the system of article numbers introduced in 1905, the last two digits indicate the size of the bear. The relationship between the sitting and standing measurements of all Teddy bears produced are as follows:

7 cm = 10 cm	10 cm = 15 cm	13 cm = 18 cm
15 cm = 22 cm	17 cm = 25 cm	20 cm = 30 cm
22 cm = 32 cm	25 cm = 35 cm	28 cm = 40 cm
32 cm = 46 cm	35 cm = 50 cm	43 cm = 60 cm
50 cm = 70 cm	80 cm = 115 cm	

Fig. 222: Lined up like a row of Russian dolls, the Teddy bears posing on this promotion photograph are arranged according to size.

THE FIRST JOINTED BEARS

Bears 28PB and 35PB are at the top of this list, of course. The 35PB is the oldest surviving representative of his family and the direct descendant of the Bear 55PB that was only made as a sample and prototype (refer to Chapter IV).

Bear 35PB supersedes the forefather of all jointed bears in March 1904, if not before. Measured standing up, he is around 50 cm tall and cords are used to attach the head and limbs to the body of the 35PB in the early days. Metal joints are also fitted in later examples and these are used exclusively for the Bear 28PB. The "Bärle PAB" with his disk-jointed limbs is already being manufactured by Steiff at the beginning of 1905, however, which implies that only a very small number of 35PBs were produced with this type of jointing.

Apart from the difference in size, the appearance of the 35PB is virtually identical to that of the 28PB offered in the Steiff catalogue from 1905 onwards, although it is highly likely that production of this bear had already commenced by the end of 1904. He measures 40 cm standing up and metal rods are used to secure his head and limbs. This is the reason for the hand-stitched seam across his head, running from one ear to the other.

Both bears are made of blond or white mohair – referred to as fine or shiny plush – and they have no voices. They are both very firmly stuffed with excelsior, have pronounced humps, long arms and legs, and fairly long, pointed muzzles. Their noses are made of sealing wax and a fine waxed thread underneath suggests the mouth. Black shoe buttons are used for the eyes and five claws are stitched onto each front and rear paw with black yarn.

According to the price list dated August 15th, 1905, the weight of the 28PB is given as 580 g and his big brother weighs in at 1050 g. Both of these Teddy bears are offered in this price list for the last time, they are no longer included in the Steiff product range for 1906.

Fig. 223: "Bärle 28 PAB" – the first bear with the appearance of the Teddy bear as we know him today.

"BÄRLE PAB" –
A PROPER CUDDLY BEAR

"Bärle PAB" (P = plush, A = angescheibt [German for disk-jointed], B = beweglich [German for movable]) was offered in seven sizes from 1905 onwards – 17, 22, 28, 35, 43, 50 and 80 cm measured sitting down – and these were supplemented by another two – 15 and 25 cm – in 1906. The standard colours are white, light brown and dark brown. There are also a number of noticeable colour deviations, such as shades of apricot or cinnamon. There are no records of these, however, and they are probably the result of irregularities in the manufacturing process that are fairly common at this time. "Bärle" does not have much in common with the first bears in the

145

PB series. While the appearance of the 55PB and both of his direct descendants is still very much oriented to the living creature on which they were modelled, the bear affectionately referred to as "Bärle" is the first one to look like a proper cuddly bear. The arms are angled less acutely, the hump is not as extremely pronounced and the muzzle has lost a great deal of its pointedness. The shoe-button eyes and stitched nose underline the generally more friendly expression on the Teddy bear's face to an even greater extent.

Early examples still have five stitched claws on each front and back paw. There is another special aspect of the new pattern, but it only occurs on a small number of the bears produced. When the contours of the individual pieces are transferred onto the material, they are positioned in such a way as to make optimum use of the mohair plush, so that as little of the precious material as possible is wasted. One width of plush is sufficient for a specific number of bears, which varies between five and more than twenty according to the size of bear. One head must be made divided into two halves, however. An additional seam is therefore necessary in the middle of the bear's head – running from the bridge of his nose right through to the back of his head – when the pieces are sewn together. Because it is seldom found, this so-called "centre seam" is much sought-after and Teddy bears with this feature are particularly popular among collectors.

But, compared with the first jointed bears, the differences are not only of a superficial nature. Disk joints are used to attach the arms, legs and head of "Bärle" to his body. Apart from that, he is stuffed with a mixture of excelsior and kapok which makes him much softer and lighter. "Bärle" 28PAB only weighs 350 g, for example, and is therefore 230 g lighter than his predecessor of the same size, the 28PB.

The weights of the "Bärle" models manufactured between 1905 and 1907 are as follows:

Art. No.					
5315 =	80 g	5317 =	90 g	5322 =	170 g
5325 =	220 g	5328 =	350 g	5335 =	610 g
5343 =	980 g	5350 =	1380 g	5380 =	5400 g

When weights are checked today, deviations of up to 20% from the original values measured at the time of manufacture are quite normal (refer to Chapter IV). Nevertheless, the differences in weight are usually less pronounced for well-preserved specimens of the "Bärle" that date back to this early period.

The catalogues from 1905 are the only ones in which the suffix "1" – used to indicate soft stuffing at the time – appears after the four-digit article numbers. If this means that kapok ceased to be used in the stuffing of the bears as early as 1906, and that they were exclusively filled with excelsior, then the weights should increase again. In spite of this, the weights quoted in the Steiff catalogues remained the same until 1908. There are several possible explanations for this: although the suffix was omitted from the article number, the bears continued to be

Fig. 224: The Teddy bear is available in 14 different sizes and three colours between 1910 and 1933. These are supplemented by numerous special models and creations.

soft-stuffed; it also seems likely that some bears were exclusively stuffed with excelsior in 1906 while production of the other softer version continued with a mixture of kapok and excelsior, i.e. both variants exist at the same time. The most likely explanation, however, is that excelsior is used as the stuffing material, but the weights quoted in the catalogues were not revised until a later date, when the growler was introduced in 1908.

The different models still around today would appear to substantiate this version of the story. The lighter, soft-filled bears are extremely difficult to find. If they have Steiff buttons in their ears at all, these are almost exclusively the blank buttons dating back to 1905/06. This same button is found just as frequently, if not more so, in the hard-filled, heavier bears.

Some of these even have five claws stitched onto their front and rear paws – further evidence of their early manufacture.

TEDDY STARTS GROWLING

1908 sees Teddy putting on weight again – and with good reason: this is the year in which growlers are first fitted into the bodies of the bears. Excelsior is exclusively used as the stuffing material again from now on, if not before, as the voice box has to be embedded securely. Apart from this, bears stuffed with just this firmer material are particularly durable and hard-wearing. Teddy's popularity no longer suffers if he puts on weight, either, because the priorities in Teddy design have changed completely since the introduction of the charming "Bärle" models. The jointed bear has finally found the right appearance, attention can now be focussed on refining the technical details.

There are no other major changes in 1908. The Steiff product range still contains the same nine sizes of bear. White, light brown and dark brown – these same mohair colours are still offered. Standard features include the shoe-button eyes to the same extent as the stitched nose and claws. The number of claws stitched onto front and rear paws is, however, reduced to four. Furthermore, bears with glass eyes are now available to order at a small extra charge.

Other sizes are not added until the following year, when article numbers 5307, 5313, 5320 and 5332 are included in the collection, supplemented by number 5310 in 1910. Augmented by these five new models, a total of fourteen different sizes are now available. And no other different sizes will be added for the next twenty years.

Production of this Teddy bear model continues in all fourteen sizes and the three standard colours right through to 1933.

Any deviations could almost be regarded as more-or-less "cosmetic" corrections. The ears move slightly closer together, for instance, and minor alterations are made to the nose. Different voices are also available for the various sizes of bear. The days of the shoe-button eyes are finally over at the beginning of the 1920s, when they are replaced by glass eyes. Each one is a clear glass bead with just a

Fig. 225:

Overalls were already being worn then, even within the Teddy family – Baho is shown here.

black pupil embedded in it – the brown colour is painted onto the reverse side. A metal loop is integrated into the glass bead and the cords used to secure the eyes to the bear's head are attached to this.

FOLLOWING THE FASHION OF THE TIME – TEDDY BEAR ON THE CATWALK

The Teddy bear is also available in different outfits. 1908 sees a complete series of differently clothed bears in the Steiff catalogue – eight to be exact. All are added to the product range in light brown, dark brown and white, the three standard colours. And the Teddies keep up with the fashion of the time, of course …

"Babad", for example, who is wearing a knitted bathing suit that is available in various different colours. He is offered in eight sizes, from 15 to 50 cm, measured sitting down, between 1908 and 1911.

"Babo", on the other hand, is wearing a felt suit and cap. The purchaser can also choose from a range of colours for his clothing. Manufactured between 1908 and 1911, Babo is only made in five sizes between 15 and 28 cm.

"Baho" is also a proper little boy, with his navy blue felt trousers held up by red straps. The elegant outfit of this bear also includes a felt cap. Baho is only available in the five sizes between 15 and 28 cm from 1908 to 1911.

A little girl finally arrived on the scene in the form of "Bagi". She is wearing a single-coloured felt ladies' suit, which can be ordered in various colours. Made in the

Fig. 226: The Babo shown here is one of the few clothed bears to have survived until the present day …

Fig. 227: Batro has also been preserved in his original clothing.

Fig. 228 left: Babo as he appears in a photograph dating back to 1908.

Fig. 229 right: Babad the Teddy bear cuts a dashing figure, even in a fashionable bathing suit.

Fig. 230: Baru, the little girl Teddy, rounds off the series of dressed bears from 1908.

Fig. 231: A real lady bear – Bagi unites style and elegance.

same colours, her stylish cap is made to match the suit. Bagi is available in the same sizes as Baho and is produced during the same period.

The little boy in the sailor suit answers to the name "Basa" and the name of his female counterpart is "Basi". She is wearing a chic navy-style dress as befitting a proper little girl at this time.

Both outfits are made in navy blue, like the matching sailors' caps. Basa and Basi are produced in the five sizes between 15 and 28 cm from 1908 to 1911.

The last little boy bear from this series of clothed Teddy bears is called "Batro" and he is wearing knitted trousers, sweater and cap with a striped pattern that is available in different colours. Batro keeps his place in the Steiff product range until 1913 and is manufactured in the five sizes mentioned above (refer to Fig. 227 on page 149).

"Baru" rounds off the she-bears in the series. She is wearing a felt smocked dress in either white, red or blue and is available in the familiar five sizes up to 1911.

All in all, the 1908 series therefore comprises eight different clothing varieties. The "Teddy G" version mentioned earlier is never offered officially in any Steiff catalogue. This clothing variant was probably never produced in series.

Fig. 232: Sailor suits are the height of fashion at the beginning of the last century. Both little boy and little girl Teddy bears must also keep abreast of the fashion.

Fig. 233: Teddy bear
with hot-water bottle.

THE HOT-WATER BOTTLE TEDDY

The Teddy bear was also required to perform a useful purpose. One of the models manufactured between 1908 and 1914 had a removable water bottle fitted inside his body. It was possible to open and close his tummy in a similar way to a lace-up closure on a boot. When the container is filled with warm water, the Teddy bear serves as a cuddly hot-water bottle.

Based on a 50 cm blond mohair Teddy bear, only 92 of these hot-water bottle Teddies were produced in total. This bear has now become one of the really rare Steiff articles and enjoys great popularity among collectors. This is also substantiated by the success of the replica of this bear that was produced in 2001. The limited edition of 3000 pieces worldwide was sold out exceptionally quickly.

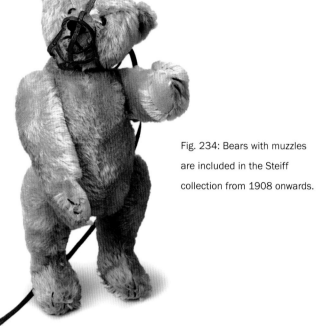

Fig. 234: Bears with muzzles are included in the Steiff collection from 1908 onwards.

TEDDY BEAR WITH MUZZLE

The jointed bear is also offered with a muzzle in the three standard colours from 1908 onwards. However, muzzles are only offered for the 22 and 25 cm bears during the first three years. The article numbers for the muzzled bears are 5315,7 and 5317,7, whereby the "7" after the comma is the only thing that distinguishes them from the numbers of the standard jointed bears. The same applies to the eight other sizes that are added to the Steiff range in 1911. Of the 14 different sizes of bear, only the three smallest and the largest model cannot be fitted with muzzles. All variants of this model are mentioned in the 1915 catalogue for the last time.

THE TUMBLING BEAR

The tumbling bear is one of the new articles in 1909. His body contains a clockwork mechanism, that is wound up by turning the arms. A little sensation: once wound up, the Teddy is then able to turn several somersaults in succession. Light brown, dark brown and white versions of the tumbling bear are available in two sizes – 18 and 23 cm – under article numbers 9318 and 9323. The light brown models remain in the collection until 1916. Light brown versions, in both sizes and with minor modifications, are added to the Steiff product range again in 1934 and production continues until 1935 (9318) and 1939 (9323) respectively.

Fig. 235: Puppets are added to the Steiff product range in the form of the Pantom bears.

A TEDDY PUPPET – THE PANTOM BEAR

The Pantom bear joins the Steiff product spectrum in 1910. Based on a development by artist Albert Schlopsnies, six threads connect the bear puppet to a wooden bar arrangement that is used to control its movements. One of these threads is also used to activate his voice.

The article numbers for the Pantom bears are 5325 P for the 35 cm version and 5328 P for the 40 cm model. This bear is only available in light brown. The smaller model is manufactured up to 1913 while production of his larger brother continues until 1918.

Fig. 236: The tumbling bear –
a clockwork mechanism enables
him to turn somersaults.

THE MOURNING BEAR – A TEDDY BEAR MADE OF BLACK PLUSH

When the "Titanic", the largest passenger steamer in the world collides with an iceberg at full speed during its maiden voyage from Southampton to New York in April 1912 and sinks within just a few hours, more than 1500 people die in the icy waters. Most of these people are British which is why an initial delivery of black plush Steiff Teddy bears is shipped to England shortly after this disaster. The so-called "mourning bears" are available in two different types of material. The short-pile plush version is only produced in 1912 and is offered in five sizes: 25, 30, 35, 40 and 50 cm, measured standing up. The second version is made of black mohair plush. He is also produced in five different sizes – 30, 35, 40, 46 and 50 cm – but continues to be available from 1912 to 1917. Black is even used for the eyes and stitching on the bear, although some examples have red felt linings behind the eyes. The same pattern is used for the mourning bears as for the standard-coloured Teddy bears, which means that there are also some extremely rare specimens with a centre seam running over their heads. One of the 50 cm mohair mourning bears (with a centre seam) is currently the most expensive bear in the world. Amounting to around £ 91,750 (more than US$ 130,000), he fetched the highest price yet paid for a Teddy bear at an official auction (also refer to Chapter IX).

DOLLY BEAR

Coloured bears were offered in the Steiff product range in 1913 for the first time. "Alfonzo", the famous red bear dating back 1908, and the blue "Emil" bear do not belong to the official Steiff collection – they are specially commissioned items/colour samples. Dolly bear is available in blue, yellow, green and red and in three sizes: 25, 30 and 32 cm measured standing up. These bears have white heads, while one of the colours mentioned above is used for their bodies. Each one has a coloured ruff around his neck and what is known as a "hug-me" voice in his tummy. Light brown yarn is used for the stitching and the shoe-button eyes are black. Production of Dolly continues until 1918. This bears have unfortunately become very rare nowadays.

Fig. 237:
One of the few surviving
Dolly bears.

Fig. 238: The black bear was issued in 1912 to mourn for the people who lost their lives when the Titanic went down.

Fig. 239: The Harlekin bear
is a sample for the coloured Steiff
bears manufactured in 1924.

Fig. 240: Teddy bear made
of a substitute material.

THE PAPER TEDDY

There are hardly any materials available for
the manufacture of plush toys in Germany at
the end of the 1st World War, not to mention
high-quality mohair plush. Steiff therefore makes
Teddy bears from a substitute material in 1919. These
bears were offered in five sizes under article numbers 5613, 5615,
5617, 5622 and 5628,2. Referred to as the "paper Teddy", this type of
bear is made from a sort of cellulose material produced from wood fibre and has a
very rough feel. Brown yarn is used for the stitching and he has black shoe-button
eyes. This bear model is manufactured in the three smaller sizes up to 1920, while
production of the two larger bears continues until 1921. The material is not very
hard-wearing, which is why there are hardly any of these bears around today.

THE COLOURED STEIFF BEARS

The "golden twenties" bring colour into life in the truest sense of the word. 1924
sees the production of red and blue Steiff Teddy bears in five sizes (18, 22, 25, 30
and 32 cm) and rosé and yellow bears in four sizes (22, 25, 30 and 32 cm). These
bears are only manufactured in very small numbers and during this year only.

Fig. 241: This rosé Teddy is
soft-filled with a mixture of
kapok and excelsior.

Firmly stuffed with excelsior, only one red-and-blue sample of this series is known to have survived. Named
Harlekin, this bear is one of the really great rare Steiff
articles (also refer to Chapter IX).

Colour returns just a year later in 1925. Red and blue are
unable to assert themselves, so bears were manufactured
in rosé and yellow instead – in three sizes initially: 33, 36
and 40 cm. The article numbers of these bears are 5323,1
K, 5326,1 K and 5330,1 K (K stands for the kapok packing). A 48 cm rosé bear with kapok filling is added to this
series a year later. The yellow version of the 48 cm bear
finally appears in 1927, but he is stuffed with excelsior.
A 51 cm version of this bear was offered in both colours
and filled with excelsior for one year only in 1927. Excel-

...sior is exclusively used for all of the bears in the coloured series from 1929 onwards. Yellow and rosé-coloured mohair is fairly sensitive to light and tends to fade rather quickly. It is therefore often difficult to recognise these bears today. A glimpse of the mohair's backing cloth, which has been dyed in the same colour, is usually sufficient to determine whether the Teddy bear in question is one of the rare examples.

Brown yarn is used to stitch the nose and claws, the eyes are made of glass painted brown on the reverse side.

TEDDY CLOWN

The Teddy Clown wears a felt clown's hat with two pompoms and a ruff around his neck. He is identical to the rosé and yellow bears described above in other respects. The sizes, article numbers and production periods of the Teddy Clown are the same, apart from the fact that he makes his debut in 1926.

Fig. 242: Music Teddy from 1928

A brown tipped version of the Teddy Clown is also available. Eleven sizes between 15 and 80 cm were offered in this mohair colour. Kapok is used to stuff the Teddy Clown during the first two years of production, but this is replaced by excelsior from 1928 until the model is discontinued in 1930.

THE MUSIC TEDDY

A version of the yellow mohair bear containing a music box is also available between 1928 and 1930. The Swiss-made mechanism is fitted inside the Music Teddy's tummy and can be made to play by pressing and releasing it continuously. This bear is only made in one size – measuring 44 cm standing up – and his article number is 5330,3.

Fig. 243: Brown-tipped
and yellow Teddy clowns.

PETSY – THE BABY BEAR

The baby bear presented under the name "Petsy" in 1928 has slightly different features from the classical Teddy bear. The glass eyes are painted blue on the reverse side, the nose and claws are stitched with red yarn, each bear has a centre seam running over its head and the large ears are reinforced by wire loops. The original Steiff catalogues only mention a brown tipped mohair version available in the ten standard sizes between 15 and 50 cm, measured sitting down. Apart from the smallest Petsy manufactured in 1928 and 1929, all other models are included in the product range until 1930. The same applies to the two sizes offered with music boxes under article numbers 5317,3 and 5320,3. Record Petsy is also produced in two sizes – 20 and 25 cm – in 1928 and 1929. Petsy continues to be manufactured as a glove puppet with and without squeaker up to as late as 1932.

Although no brass-coloured Petsy is mentioned in any Steiff catalogue, a sample in this colour has been preserved in the Steiff archives and examples of the so-called "Petsy Messing" [brass Petsy] turn up in the collectors' market now and again. It therefore seems very likely that at least a small number of brass-coloured Petsy bears were manufactured in series.

Apart from these, a few isolated white mohair models of Petsy are known among collectors. These are so rare, however, that they would appear to be samples or specially commissioned items.

Fig. 244: A standard version of Petsy, the bear baby, made of brown-tipped mohair.

Fig. 245 bottom left: A Petsy made of white mohair is very seldom found.

Fig. 246 bottom: The brass-coloured Petsy is not listed in any catalogue.

Fig. 247: Two sizes of Petsy are also offered with carriage that moves automatically when pulled and automatic voice under the designation Record Petsy.

Fig. 248: Teddy baby with teeth.

Fig. 249: The names given to the clothed versions were Teddy Baby "Maid & Bub".

Fig. 250: Teddy Baby with mouth closed.

TEDDY BABY

Baby bear Petsy is followed by Teddy Baby a year later. Even the bears produced in the first series in 1929 differ considerably from the Teddy bears manufactured up to this time. The rear paws or feet have now been shaped in such a way as to enable this bear to stand up on his own. Furthermore, close-cropped plush is used on the top of each foot. The felt paw inserts are sewn underneath and give the Teddy Baby an even more gawky appearance. The muzzle is also made of short-pile plush and is therefore fitted separately during the manufacturing process. All of the 1929 models have closed mouths and are made of maize-coloured or dark brown mohair, or maize-coloured wool plush. They are available in 6 sizes – 15, 20, 25, 30, 38 and 45 cm, measured standing up – and all of their article numbers begin with a "6". Some of these bears are still included in the Steiff collection until 1932.

A few rare examples are made from yellow or rosé-coloured mohair in three different sizes. The article numbers of these are 6323,2, 6330,2 and 6336,2. Although as many as 272 rosé and 264 yellow Teddy Babies were made, not a single one has been discovered in today's collectors' market up to now.

One very special model is the Teddy Baby with open mouth and teeth with article number 6329,2 that was produced between 1929 and 1930. Only 25 of these bears were manufactured in total and one of these has been preserved in the Steiff archives. And finally, there were two clothed models of the 25 cm, maize-coloured mohair Teddy Baby: 357 of the Teddy Baby "Bub" (boy) and 354 of the Teddy Baby "Maid" (girl) were clothed on the Steiff premises.

Fig. 251: Versions of the Teddy Baby with open mouth were also made from wool plush for a short time.

The further developed model of the Teddy Baby is presented in 1930. Although the smaller new additions to the Teddy bear family – 9, 12 and 13 cm tall – still have closed mouths, their larger relations – 15 cm and above – have open mouths, giving the Teddy Babies an even cuter appearance. Available in a total of twelve different sizes – 9 to 45 cm measured standing up – these bears are made of white, maize-coloured or dark brown mohair. Their article numbers all begin with a "7". The colour white remains in the product spectrum until 1933, whereas production of some sizes of maize-coloured and dark brown Teddy Babies continues right through to the end of the 1950s.

In 1941, dark brown Teddy Babies measuring 65 cm are made as showpieces, to be followed by 150 cm tall bears around 1960.

Teddy Babies of the same three standard colours are also available in wool plush. This material was not used any later than 1932, however. The smallest wool plush bears measure 15 cm, but the smallest white bear is 20 cm tall.

Fig. 252: Teddy Baby bears
with open mouths are available
from 1930 onwards.

Fig. 253: Dicky Bear is presented as a new item in white or blond mohair in 1931.

DICKY BEAR

Presented as a new article in 1931, Dicky bear is produced in blond or white and also has an inset muzzle made of short-pile mohair and a smiling expression on his face, created by means of decorative painting. His paw linings and the soles of his feet are made of velvet initially, printed with a pattern that corresponds to the markings on the inner surface of a front paw and the undersurface of a hind paw. Plain felt is used for the paw linings and soles of later models. Both colours are offered in 12 sizes between 15 and 75 cm measured standing up.

Fig. 254: Life is never boring in the Teddy family.

The blond bears measuring 32 and 35 cm are included in the product range for the longest, being manufactured right up until 1937.

Two sizes of the same bear are also made from dark brown wool plush from 1935 onwards. Article numbers 5532 and 5543 (the new method of measuring was introduced in 1934, i.e. the size quoted in places 3 and 4 of the article number correspond to the height of the standing bear) remain in the collection until 1941 (32 cm) and 1940 (43 cm) respectively. A third model of this design measuring 25 cm is only available between 1939 and 1941.

The Teddy bears are measured in a standing position again from 1934 onwards and the article numbers change accordingly. Thirteen sizes of Teddy bear from 10 to 75 cm are available at this time in three colours: blond (previously referred to as light brown), white and dark brown.

Fig. 255: Dicky is not made from dark brown wool plush until 1935.

There are no other major changes in the bear's appearance – the Teddy bear still resembles the model dating back to between 1908 and 1933 with a few minor modifications.

Fig. 256: Blond Teddy Baby
made of synthetic silk plush
dating back to around 1948.

TEDDY BEARS MADE OF SYNTHETIC SILK PLUSH

Materials became scarce again at Steiff during the 2nd World War and for some time afterwards. Bears and other animals were made of synthetic silk plush this time, but this substitute material doesn't prove to be very hard-wearing either. Although extremely pretty with a wonderful silky gloss in mint condition, it soon becomes shabby after just a few childhood romps. As a result, only perfect examples of these bears attract the majority of collectors, in spite of them being so rare.

A NEW DESIGN CHANGES THE BEAR WORLD – THE ORIGINAL TEDDY

The name "Original Teddy" was first used as a designation for the Teddy bear by Margarete Steiff GmbH after the 2nd World War. Steiff is already able to resume delivery of Teddy bears of the usual quality as early as 1949. And a model with a completely different design is presented just a year later in 1950: the arms and legs are shorter, the head is round, the muzzle too, and the hump has virtually disappeared from Teddy's back. This "Original Teddy" is available in a total of 12 sizes between 10 and 75 cm and four colours: gold (corresponding to blond), caramel, dark brown and white. It remains part of the Steiff collection until 1966, when it is superseded by the so-called mask-type bear, who was given this name because his short-pile mohair face looked rather like a mask. The mask-type bear is the first Teddy to be filled with synthetic stuffing materials from the end of the 1960s onwards. His external appearance has been updated compared with his predecessors, and it has been adapted to suit modern tastes. He then remains unaltered in the product range as the "Original Teddy" for almost 30 years leading up to 1993.

Fig. 257: Dark brown mohair
Teddy bear from 1949.

Fig. 258: The mask-type bear
is a new item in 1966 and
remains in the Steiff collection
until 1993.

Fig. 259: A completely
revised model of the Teddy
bear is presented in 1950.

Fig. 260: Jackie,
my very own personal
favourite.

JACKIE –
THE JUBILEE TEDDY

The Teddy bear doesn't celebrate his 50th birthday until 1953. This is because, at the time, the
jubilee is not referred to the date of the first jointed bear's creation, but the date on
which the Bear 55PB was registered at Heidenheim district court in 1903. Jackie
is offered in three sizes between 1953 and 1955: 17, 25 and 35 cm. In addition to
these, a few 75 cm versions were produced as showpieces. The Jubilee Teddy
becomes a very popular bear and has been known to fetch prices in excess of
US$ 15,000 at auctions.

There is great diversity in the range of Steiff Teddy bears produced over the
last 100 years. The last 30 years have seen the introduction of modern
materials for the bear's fur coat and filling, enabling the emergence of completely
new creations. There is virtually no end to the colour spectrum now available, the
designers never cease to be inspired by the new possibilities that have opened up.
So, there is no need to worry about the Teddy bear's design prospects for the
future – he's certainly not ready for the scrap heap yet, even if he is 100 years old.
Quite the contrary: he keeps his youthful appearance continuously and goes with
the times.
The high regard shown to the original models – both precious originals and the
faithful copies that have been produced as replicas since 1980 – is further evidence
in favour of Teddy's youthfulness in spite of his age. And the radiant expressions
that still appear in the eyes of children and adults alike when they see a Teddy bear
allow us to hope for the best when it comes to his future.

Fig. 261: Jackie – the jubilee
Teddy issued to celebrate the
Teddy bear's 50th anniversary.

Appendix

Utility model registrations – Translations

Column headings:

Column 1: Serial No.

Column 2: Applicant's name or company

Column 3: Date and time of registration

Column 4: Designation of the registered utility or design model

Column 5: Information indicating whether the article is for use in 2 or 3-dimensional products

Column 6: Period of protection

Column 7: Extension to the period of protection

Fig. 28

Line 1

Column 1: 88.1.,

Column 2: Margarete Steiff, Filzspielwaren-fabrik (felt toy factory) in Giengen / Brenz

Column 3: 13th July 1903, 9 o'clock in the morning

Column 4: A sealed package containing 18 different 3-dimensional products, toys in the form of animals and human beings, painted and covered with various fabrics Kamel M. Bär 55 PB. Aff 60 PB. Überdax M. Ele 14 T. Eich 5 M Blatt. Fox 17 siz T. Frosch Nad. Has 14 ren T. Hen Brut. Kaz 12 lig T. Kaz 14 T. Kaz 14 siz T. Lam 22 T. Postmann 35. Post-mann 50. Police 50. Sau 14 T.

Column 5: 3-dimensional products

Column 6: 3 years

Line 2

Column 1: 2.,

Column 2: Margarete Steiff in Giengen / Br.

Column 3: 28th June 1906, 10 o'clock in the morning

Column 4: Kamel M, Bär 55 PB. Aff 60 PB, Überdax M, Hen Brut, Lam 22 T, Postmann 35, Post-mann 50.

Column 5: „ (ditto)

Column 6: –

Column 7: 3 years

Note concerning line 2, column 4:

This means that the period of protection was only extended for another 3 years for those articles that are mentioned again in Column 4 / No. 88.2.

Fortlaufende Nr.	Name bezw. Firma des Anmeldenden.	Tag und Stunde der Anmeldung.	Bezeichnung des angemeldeten Musters oder Modells.	Angabe: ob das Muster für Flächenerzeugnisse oder für plastische Erzeugnisse bestimmt ist.	Schutzfrist.	Verlängerung der Schutzfrist.
1.	2.	3.	4.	5.	6.	7.
88. 1.	_Margarete Steiff_, Filzspielwarenfabrik in Giengen a/Brz	13. Juli 1903 vormittags 1 Uhr	ein versiegeltes Packet enthaltend 18 ver= schiedene plastische Erzeugnisse, bemerkt u nicht ausfführ... Steffen ... Spielsachen in Gestalt ... Tieren u. Menschen. Kamel 16 / Bär 55 P.B / 44 60 P.B. Elephant 16 Elef. 14 J. Erich 5 16 Matt. Foxl 17 5 J. Brumb... Elad Was 14 v. 28. Hen Bräc. Kaz 10 lig J. Kaz 14 J. Kaz 16 18 J Lam 22 J. Postmann 35 Post= mann 50 + Polce 50 Sal 14 J.	plastische Er= zeugnisse.	3 Jahre	
2.	_Margarete Steiff_ in Giengen a/Brz	28. Juni 1906 vorm. 10 Uhr	Kamel 16 Bär 55 P.B. 44 60 P.B. Elephant 16 Hen Bräc. Lam 22 J. Postmann 35 Post= mann 50	4	—	drei Jahre

Utility model registrations – Translations

Column headings:

Column 1: Serial No.

Column 2: Applicant's name or company

Column 3: Date and time of registration

Column 4: Designation of the registered utility or design model

Column 5: Information indicating whether the article is for use in 2 or 3-dimensional products

Column 6: Period of protection

Column 7: Extension to the period of protection

Fig. 32

Line 1

Column 1: 86.1.,

Column 2: Margarete Steiff, Filzspielwaren-fabrik (felt toy factory) in Giengen / Brenz

Column 3: 9th August 1902, 6 o'clock in the afternoon

Column 4: A sealed package containing 5 different toys in the form of animals and human beings, painted and covered with various fabrics
Works number
Police 703580
Police 705080
Footballer 703581
Neger 703582
Ruderer / Frosch / 703585

Column 5: 3-dimensional products

Column 6: 3 years

Line 2

Column 1: 2.,

Column 2: „ (ditto)

Column 3: 3rd July 1905

Column 4: as above

Column 5: „ (ditto)

Column 6: –

Column 7: 3 years

Note concerning line 2, column 4:

This means that the period of protection was extended for another 3 years for all of the articles mentioned in Column 4 / No. 86.1.

Fortlaufende Nr.	Name bezw. Firma des Anmeldenden.	Tag und Stunde der Anmeldung.	Bezeichnung des angemeldeten Musters oder Modells.	Angabe: ob das Muster für Flächenerzeugnisse oder für plastische Erzeugnisse bestimmt ist.	Schutzfrist.	Verlängerung der Schutzfrist.
1.	2.	3.	4.	5.	6.	7.
86. 1.	Margarete Steiff, Filzspielwarenfabrik in Giengen a/Brz.	9. Aug. 1902 nachmitt. 6 Uhr.	ein versiegeltes Paket, enthaltend 5 verschiedene, bemalte u. mit verschiedenen Stoffen bekleidete Spielsachen in Gestalt von Menschen u. Tieren. Fabriknummern: Polizei 703580, " 705080, Footballer 703581, Neger 703582. Kladderadatsch (Frosch) 703585.	plastische Erzeugnisse.	3 Jahre	
2.	"	3. Juli 1905	desgleichen	"	—	3 Jahre

Utility model registrations – Translations

Column headings:

Column 1: Serial No.
Column 2: Applicant's name or company
Column 3: Date and time of registration
Column 4: Designation of the registered utility or design model
Column 5: Information indicating whether the article is for use in
2 or 3-dimensional products
Column 6: Period of protection
Column 7: Extension to the period of protection

Fig. 53

Line 1

Column 1: 94.
Column 2: Margarete Steiff, Filzspielwaren-
fabrik (felt toy factory) in Giengen /
Brenz
Column 3: 5th March 1904, 3 o'clock in the
afternoon
Column 4: Toys in the form of animals and
human beings, painted and
covered with various fabrics.
Works number
Bär 35 PB, Esl 43 P.B.
Ele 35 PB, Dax 20 M ohne R.
Fox jung 22 T, Fox jung 17 T.,
Kaz 8 lig T, Kaz 12 lig T. sitz.
Kaz 12 siz M, Häng Bulk T,
Häng Hask T, Häng Kazk T,
Häng Lamk T, Offizier 35 franz,
Soldat 35 franz, Soldat 50 engl.,
Soldat 35 engl., Onkel Sam 50,
Foxy Grandpa 35, Foxy Boy 22,
Happy holigan 35, Gaston
americ 50, Police 35 americ,
Police 50 americ, Ste-Narr 17
Fox 12 siz T., Ent mit Musik,
Police 100 amerik.,
Clown 100 engl., Clown 100 bel.,
Clown 100 am., Clown 100
sax, Clown 100 ba, Clown
100 sam.
Column 5: 3-dimensional products
Column 6: 3 years

Line 2

Column 1: „ (ditto)
Column 2: Margarete Steiff GmbH
in Giengen / Br.
Column 3: 20th February 1907, 3 o'clock in
the afternoon
Column 4: refer to the application
files for utility model reg. Upd.
Column 5: „ (ditto)
Column 6: –
Column 7: 3 years

Note concerning line 2, column 4:

This means that the period of protection was
extended for another 3 years for all of the
articles mentioned in Column 4 / No. 94 that
are not underlined (articles to which the
extension does not apply were underlined in
order to maintain legibility).

Fortlaufende Nr.	Name bezw. Firma des Anmeldenden.	Tag und Stunde der Anmeldung.	Bezeichnung des angemeldeten Musters oder Modells.	Angabe: ob das Muster für Flächenerzeugnisse oder für plastische Erzeugnisse bestimmt ist.	Schutzfrist.	Verlängerung der Schutzfrist.
1.	2.	3.	4.	5.	6.	7.
94.	_Margarette Steiff, Filzspielwarenfabrik in Giengen_	5. März 1897, nachmittags 3 Uhr	_Bemalte mit verschiedenen Stoffen überzogene Spielfiguren in Gestalt von Tieren u. Menschen. Fabrikationsnummer: Bär 35 PB, Esel 43 S u. ... Ele 35 PB, Dar 28 ... Fox jung 22 T, Foxjung 17 T, Kas 8 lig T, Kas 13 lig T, Kas 12 ... King Rüll T, King Bask T, King Capt T, King Lank T, Offizier 35 franz, Soldat 35 franz, Solo ... Soldat 35 engl, Onkel Sam 51, Foxy Grandpa 35, Fox ... Happy Hooligan 35, Gassen ... amerie 50, Polio 35 amerie, Polio 51 amerie, Holar 17 Fox 12 sitz T, Ente mit Küken Police 100 amerik, Clown 100 engl, Clown 100 bl, Clown 100 am, Clown 100 sax, Clown 100 ba, ... 100 am._	_plastische für zwei Jahre._	_Drei Jahre._	
4	_Margarette Steiff, Inn. ... in Giengen_	20. Februar 1897 nachmittags 3 Uhr	_s. Eintrag L 239 der Mustertabelle Abb._	4	—	_Drei Jahre_

Index

Sources of photographic material

DaimlerChrysler Corporate Archives	6
GAF Günther Pfeiffer GmbH	1, 2, 15, 21, 37-41, 44, 46-48, 50-52, 54, 60, 62, 67, 71-90, 92, 100, 101, 113, 116, 122, 128, 129, 131-152, 154, 155, 157-162, 164-177, 179-182, 184-191, 193-196, 199-201, 203-208, 210-212, 214-217, 220, 223, 224, 226, 227, 233-253, 255-261
Heimann Systems GmbH	36, 42, 43, 55, 66
Margarete Steiff GmbH	3-5, 7-14, 16-20, 22-35, 45, 49, 53, 56-59, 61, 63-65, 68-70, 91, 93-99, 102-112, 114, 115, 117-121, 123-127, 130, 153, 156, 163, 178, 198, 202, 209, 213, 218, 219, 221, 222, 225, 228-232, 254
Doll's House Museum Basel	183
Teddy Bears of Witney	192, 197

Acknowledgements

On behalf of Margarete Steiff GmbH and myself, I would like to take this opportunity to say thank you to everybody who has contributed towards producing this book. A special thank you goes to Gigi Oeri, Jürgen Hubbert, Thomas Lo and Ian Pout, who were kind enough to give us all an insight into the stories behind their own very personal "collectivitis".

Günther Pfeiffer